Cambridge El

C000163114

Elements in Bioethics an
edited by
Thomasine Kushner
California Pacific Medical Center, San Francisco

CONTROLLING LOVE

The Ethics and Desirability of Using 'Love Drugs'

Peter Herissone-Kelly
University of Central Lancashire, Preston

CAMBRIDGE
UNIVERSITY PRESS

Shaftesbury Road, Cambridge CB2 8EA, United Kingdom

One Liberty Plaza, 20th Floor, New York, NY 10006, USA

477 Williamstown Road, Port Melbourne, VIC 3207, Australia

314–321, 3rd Floor, Plot 3, Splendor Forum, Jasola District Centre,
New Delhi – 110025, India

103 Penang Road, #05–06/07, Visioncrest Commercial, Singapore 238467

Cambridge University Press is part of Cambridge University Press & Assessment,
a department of the University of Cambridge.

We share the University's mission to contribute to society through the pursuit of
education, learning and research at the highest international levels of excellence.

www.cambridge.org
Information on this title: www.cambridge.org/9781009299053

DOI:10.1017/9781009299060

First published 2022

A catalogue record for this publication is available from the British Library.

ISBN 978-1-009-29905-3 Paperback
ISSN 2752-3934 (online)
ISSN 2752-3926 (print)

Cambridge University Press & Assessment has no responsibility for the persistence
or accuracy of URLs for external or third-party internet websites referred to in this
publication and does not guarantee that any content on such websites is, or will
remain, accurate or appropriate.

Every effort has been made in preparing this Element to provide accurate and up-to-date
information which is in accord with accepted standards and practice at the time of
publication. Although case histories are drawn from actual cases, every effort has been
made to disguise the identities of the individuals involved. Nevertheless, the authors,
editors, and publishers can make no warranties that the information contained herein is
totally free from error, not least because clinical standards are constantly changing
through research and regulation. The authors, editors, and publishers therefore disclaim
all liability for direct or consequential damages resulting from the use of material
contained in this Element. Readers are strongly advised to pay careful attention to
information provided by the manufacturer of any drugs or equipment that they
plan to use.

Controlling Love

The Ethics and Desirability of Using 'Love Drugs'

Elements in Bioethics and Neuroethics

DOI: 10.1017/9781009299060
First published online: August 2022

Peter Herissone-Kelly
University of Central Lancashire, Preston

Author for correspondence: Peter Herissone-Kelly, pnherissone-kelly@uclan.ac.uk

Abstract: Recent research in neurochemistry has shown there to be a number of chemical compounds that are implicated in the patterns of lust, attraction, and attachment that undergird romantic love. For example, there is evidence that the phenomenon of attachment is associated with the action of oxytocin and vasopressin. There is therefore some reason to suppose that patterns of lust, attraction, and attachment could be regulated via manipulation of these substances in the brain: in other words, by their use as 'love drugs'. A growing bioethical literature asks searching questions about this prospect, and especially about the use of such drugs to enhance or reignite attachment in flagging relationships. This Element examines some of the central arguments on the topic and sounds a note of caution. It urges that there are reasons to think the states of attachment produced or facilitated by the use of such drugs would not be desirable.

Keywords: love drugs, authenticity, neuroethics, oxytocin, love

ISBNs: 9781009299053 (PB), 9781009299060 (OC)
ISSNs: 2752-3934 (online), 2752-3926 (print)

Contents

1 Introduction

As students of popular song know, love is a many-splendoured thing; it is all you need and certainly what the world needs now; it is like a butterfly, as soft and gentle as a sigh. Unfortunately, it is also like a butterfly in its tendency not to stay in place for too long and to fly away without warning. Sooner or later, love may well peter out, and in doing so it will tear us apart again. Many of us accord romantic love a central place in our lives, yet we appear to have little control over its presence in them.

This sorry state of affairs may be on the brink of changing. In the opinion of some thinkers, the fact that scientists have begun successfully to identify the neurochemicals and brain processes associated with the various stages of romantic love means we are facing the prospect of bringing those stages under greater control. If our relationships are fading, it may soon be possible to reinvigorate them through pharmaceutical interventions, used perhaps in combination with more conventional relationship therapy. One way of doing this might be by exogenous administration of the neurochemicals that are produced endogenously when we are in the grip of love.

The biological anthropologist Helen Fisher sees love as having three phases: lust, attraction, and attachment.[1] Lust drives us to seek out any appropriate partner for mating: it is not focussed on a particular person, but has, so to speak, a diffuse object. Attraction narrows our attention down to a particular individual and is typically associated with the early, more passionate stages of a relationship. Attachment represents the formation and maintenance of a stable pair bond and is thus associated with the more settled phase of a relationship, after the decline of the initial, tempestuous chapter.[2] Each of those phases, research shows, is associated with its own brain systems and its own set of neurotransmitters or hormones. For example, testosterone is implicated in lust; norepinephrine and dopamine in attraction; and oxytocin and vasopressin in attachment. If we were deliberately and appropriately to administer such substances, then, the hope is that we could manipulate the higher-level romantic phenomena with which they are associated, bringing those phenomena in line with our preferences and values. So, for instance, a couple who value their relationship, but find it to be steadily fading, may be able to rescue it with – alongside relationship counselling perhaps – carefully targeted pharmaceutical remedies. So-called 'love drugs' could help us to meet our preferences and achieve what we value in relationships.

That prospect fills some with jubilation but is apt to make others feel decidedly uneasy. Is it ethically permissible to manipulate our romantic neuro-machinery in this way? If it is permissible, is it also desirable? Philosophical inquiry into such issues is still relatively young. Any attempt to get to grips with it needs not only to take into account, but primarily to concentrate on, the agenda-setting writings of a small group of co-authors that clusters around the Oxford moral philosopher Julian Savulescu. The most frequent of Savulescu's collaborators in this area is Brian D. Earp, but other contributors to their work have been Anders Sandberg (who, in 2008, co-wrote with Savulescu the first of the group's papers on this topic[3]), and the psychologists Olga A. Wudarczyk and Adam Guastella. In what follows, I will refer to this group, and its various subsets, as 'the authors' or 'our authors'.

While the authors' earlier work on the topic tends to focus on what we might call, coining a phrase, endomimetic love drugs (by which I shall mean exogenously administered doses of love-associated neurochemicals that are endogenously produced), their output as a whole is not restricted to concern with such substances. The extension of the expression 'love drugs' is, in their hands, extraordinarily wide. They take it to mean, roughly, any drug at all that affects lust, attraction, or attachment. SSRIs, for example, can be categorized as love drugs on this understanding, since ridding a partner of depression may enable a relationship to get back on track.[4] Viagra is sometimes classified as a love drug by our authors,[5] and sometimes not,[6] though when it is, it is on the assumption that engaging in a certain style of sexual activity may contribute to the health of a relationship.

In their most recent work, starting with Earp and Savulescu's 2020 book *Love Is the Drug: The Chemical Future of Our Relationships*,[7] the authors' emphasis has shifted towards the use of psychedelics (both classic psychedelics such as LSD and psilocybin, and entactogens such as MDMA) in the context of relationship therapy. This is, strictly speaking, only a shift in emphasis – MDMA is mentioned in passing in Savulescu and Sandberg's initial paper[8] – but it is nonetheless a seismic one, and one that seems to have modified their stance somewhat. When they were concerned chiefly with the issue of endomimetic love drugs, their conclusion, or part of that conclusion, was straightforwardly that use of love drugs would be desirable: something that people in appropriate circumstances would have good reason to undertake. As psychedelics have crept softly centre stage in their work, the stance has become that we have good reason, not yet to *use* love drugs, but to carry out research into their efficacy and safety. This reflects a developing position in contemporary psychiatry, which maintains that while psychedelics show considerable potential for a range of legitimate therapeutic applications, much more research is needed before we can confidently and routinely deploy them.[9]

Our authors also argue for the use, in certain contexts, of what they call antilove drugs: chemicals that might be able to quell unwanted or inappropriate passions, disrupting, for example, attachment to abusive partners.[10] A substance may count as an anti-love drug even though it is not deliberately employed to quash romance. For example, an unfortunate side effect of SSRIs in a small number of patients is the blunting of the feelings of empathy and concern essential to a healthy romantic relationship.[11]

Some philosophers have objected that the expression 'anti-love drugs' is a misnomer, given a number of the applications that Savulescu and his colleagues have in mind for the substances so named. For example, it is at least possible (though controversial) to question whether the person who is emotionally dependent upon an abusive partner feels, specifically, *love* for that partner.[12] In addition, the authors regard the combatting of paedophilic urges as an application of anti-love drugs; as Andrew McGee points out, it is surely inaccurate to suggest that what is being extinguished in such a case is anything we would want to describe as love (the etymology of the expression 'paedo-philia' notwithstanding).[13] What is more, Robbie Arrell has disputed whether the sort of deadening of feeling that on rare occasions accompanies SSRI use entails a concomitant dimming of an agent's love for a partner.[14]

In order to keep matters manageable in the current work, I will only be considering questions about the use of love drugs; I will not also cover the use of so-called 'anti-love drugs'. Nor will I be addressing the use of everything that our authors would count as a love drug. The deployment of some medica-tions in the way they envisage seems to me to be largely unproblematic and so not to warrant a great deal of scrutiny. If treating someone with an SSRI alleviates their depression and allows them to re-engage with a partner, then the intervention seems essentially to be a 'ground-clearing' exercise. That is, it removes an external impediment to what would otherwise be a well-functioning relationship. There is no manipulation of love here, only the opportunity to give it free rein. The use of psychedelics as love drugs is more controversial. Since our authors commit themselves only to the view that it merits further research, and since it is worthy of much more consideration than I have space to give it here, I leave the topic to one side.

My attention in what follows will fall, then, exclusively on our authors' arguments for the use of endomimetic love drugs. One reason for this focus is that the use of such drugs may appear at first sight to be less controversial than the use of other substances for the same purpose. The clue here lies in my neologism 'endomimetic'. Ingestion of, say, oxytocin via a nasal spray mimics what happens when people gain or strengthen a romantic attachment in more time-honoured ways. In fact, even to talk of mimicry here is potentially misleading. The effects in the two cases – the 'natural' case and the case where a deliberate pharmaceutical intervention is undertaken – are identical. The brain undergoes exactly the same chemical changes in each. Only the aetiology differs: any imitation ends once administration is complete. It may be difficult to see, then, how there can be any moral difference between the two types of case (assuming that certain ethical thresholds are met in the situation in which love drugs are taken, for example, that informed consent on the part of the drug users is present) or why one case might be desirable and the other not. Perhaps, as our authors write: 'There is no morally relevant difference between marriage therapy, a massage, a glass of wine, a fancy pink, steamy potion and a pill. All act at the biological level to make the release of substances like oxytocin and dopamine more likely.'[15] There is, admittedly, something not *quite* right about what Savulescu and Sandberg say here. If the pill or the steamy potion (or the nasal spray) contain oxytocin, taking them does not simply *increase the likelihood* of oxytocin being in the system, in the way that a massage might. Still, the neurochemical outcome will be the same as when the stars align, and the massage happens to work its magic. If there is nothing wrong with the use of massage, it is perhaps difficult to see how there could be anything wrong with the administration of exogenous oxytocin. Both are means of introducing oxytocin to the system. It is just that one is more reliable and direct than the other.

It is precisely here, perhaps, that an objection may be raised. As just suggested, the deliberate administration of oxytocin does rather more than make the presence of oxytocin in the brain more probable. It consequently gives *greater* control over our romantic machinery than, say, the use of massage or the sharing of a bottle of wine. As we shall see in Section 3, when we come to reject a position that I call 'isolated-state reductionism', increased control over one aspect of our romantic machinery does not automatically produce increased control over romantic attachment, since on any plausible picture a whole range of neural factors need to co-operate for attachment to be formed or strengthened. But still, we might feel that the greater control that accompanies the use of endomimetic love drugs creates ethical issues or questions about the value of the resulting state, which are absent in the more 'natural' cases.

Our authors appear to concede that there could be such a thing as undue control over our romantic lives,[16] though they are vague about precisely why some levels of control would count as excessive, and where the threshold lies between acceptable and unacceptable levels. Nonetheless, they seem convinced that, wherever that threshold is to be found, the use of endomimetic love drugs is extremely unlikely to cross it. There is, they point out, a wide spectrum of conceivable levels of manipulation between those offered by traditional, rather hit-and-miss means of attempting to secure attachment, on the one hand, and full-blown mind control on the other.[17] Love drugs would provide greater control than traditional means (or traditional means alone), otherwise there would be no point in taking them. But they would not deliver a problematic degree of control.

We might wonder, as Michael Hauskeller does,[18] how the authors know this, especially since they offer no criteria for when a desirable, or at least palatable, measure of control would tip over into the realm of the excessive. However, and very importantly, by the end of the current work I hope to show that the *degree* of control provided by love drugs is not the issue that should primarily concern us; we should feel more uneasy about the *kind* of control they may put in our hands. Indeed, our authors appear to notice something of this sort at one point, in their characterization of what would be wrong with a love potion that could conjure attraction from scratch:

> Note that the goal . . . is not to kindle some arbitrary attraction out of thin air like love potions do in fairy tales, but to help existing love survive the test of time. Scientists do not yet understand the attraction system well enough to allow us to conjecture whether love potions of the fairy-tale variety are even possible. And even if they were, they would pose a number of moral problems since they would create inauthentic relationships with no real grounding in the actual compatibilities of the individuals involved. In contrast, our arguments examined the possibility of using love drugs to make *authentic* relationships last.[19]

The problem with quasi-magically creating romantic attraction *ex nihilo*, then, is not so much that it would involve the wielding of an excess of control, but that the control wielded would be of an inappropriate sort. It would be such as to create an inauthentic relationship, a relationship not founded in a genuine compatibility or, we might say, on genuine *reasons*. This latter way of putting the problem will prove to be very important to an argument I will advance towards the end of this Element.

The quoted passage also partially explains why our authors for the most part (and especially as time progresses) steer clear of recommending or suggesting that we might use love drugs to induce new relationships. Instead, their emphasis is on using pharmaceuticals (or, in the case of psychedelics, looking carefully at the case for using them) to help bolster flagging relationships, in which Fisher's third phase of love – attachment – is diminishing or has been largely or completely extinguished. Accordingly, in addition to focussing on endomimetic love drugs and eschewing consideration of anti-love drugs, the current Element will concentrate exclusively on their prospective use in rejuvenating attachment in existing relationships.

I will start, in the next section, by setting out our authors' core argument for the use of (some, non-psychedelic) love drugs, including endomimetics, in order to strengthen attachment. That done, I will, in Section 3, take a closer look at the claim, essential to the core argument, that the action of certain neurochemicals is *associated* with the phenomena of love and attachment. I will note that in advancing this claim, our authors are eager to avoid a number of different forms of reductionism and to do so in order to quell two concerns that might make us reluctant to embrace the use of love drugs.

In Section 4, I will explain that there appear to be two distinct accounts of the action of neurochemicals such as oxytocin to be found in both the scientific and the ethical literature. I call these the productive account and the facilitative account. According to the former, oxytocin can, when certain enabling conditions are in place, produce or strengthen attachment directly. According to the latter, what is directly produced or strengthened by the action of oxytocin is not attachment, but some mental state or behavioural repertoire that provides fertile ground for the development or deepening of attachment, while not compelling it. I will conclude that, for the purposes of a work such as this one, we can afford to be agnostic about whether the productive or the facilitative account is correct, since both give us reason to suspect that the use of endomimetic love drugs would not be desirable.

In Section 5, I will investigate the possibility that there is some sort of tension between the object (in the sense of 'focus') of romantic love, and the object (in the sense of 'purpose') of someone's taking love drugs. I will conclude that often there may be, though we can easily envisage circumstances – which therefore would be the best sorts of circumstances in which endomimetic love drugs could be used – where there would not. Even so, it is not obvious, given what I go on to say in Section 6, that these best circumstances would thereby count as ideal or unproblematic.

In that section, I will ask whether the states that would result from the use of endomimetic love drugs, even when used in the best possible circumstances, could authentically qualify as love or could provide a foundation on which a genuine love might be built. Relatedly, the following question will be posed: does the object of an attachment strengthened through the use of endomimetic love drugs have reason to value that attachment, and does its subject have reason to endorse it? I will list three possible outcomes of taking endomimetic love drugs. If either one of the first two possibilities is actual, the state produced will not count as authentic love, nor will it provide a plausible basis for such love. If, on the other hand, the third possibility is actual, then the state produced may either be, or constitute fertile ground for, authentic love. Nonetheless, couples who use love drugs would have no way of *knowing* that the third possibility is actual and so would be inescapably uncertain about whether the state they find themselves in is authentic love or not.

In the investigation that follows, a couple of key strategies will be adopted. First, I will accept as beyond question that there is some correlation between neural goings-on (the release of certain hormones, the activation of certain neural pathways, and so on) on the one hand, and higher-level romantic phenomena on the other. Secondly, we need to bear in mind that the purpose of using love drugs is not *ultimately* to bring about certain chemical changes in the user, but to do so only as a means of producing or making room for characteristic romantic phenomena, our knowledge of which precedes (or may precede) any awareness of their neural underpinnings. In other words, in taking love drugs at all, it is *love as we have always known it, and as we have always valued it*, that we are concerned to produce or enable. That being the case, we will be concerned to 'save the appearances' where love is concerned. If pharmaceutical intervention leads either to our coming to understand love in a manner incompatible with the features of love that we value, or for some reason necessarily fails to produce those features, then such intervention will undermine its own goals.

My conclusion will be that we have cause to be circumspect about the prospective use of endomimetic love drugs. There are reasons to suppose that the states of attachment produced or facilitated by their use would not be desirable, either for their subjects or for their objects. That is, they either would not count as authentic love and so would not be the states at which agents would aim in taking love drugs, or, while they would count as authentic love, there would always be sufficient reason for their subjects and objects to question their authenticity. At the very least, I want to suggest that the optimism our authors display concerning endomimetic love drugs is premature. There are pressing issues that cry out for consideration before we can confidently endorse the use of such substances, and the authors either do not entertain those issues or, insofar as they do, neglect to give them their due weight.

It will be noted that my conclusion appears simply to be one concerning the probable *undesirability* of using endomimetic love drugs. It may be pointed out that to pronounce their use undesirable is not necessarily to maintain that it would be unethical. This is true, given a certain narrow understanding of the expression 'unethical'. It may not be morally impermissible for someone to take a substance that either does not produce the results they are aiming at in taking it or will leave them inescapably uncertain that those results are in place. Of course, it may be unethical to market it as delivering results that, in fact, it cannot produce (or, for all its users know, may not produce) or to engage in costly research into the production of outcomes that there is no good reason for anyone to desire.

In addition, though, there is a wider understanding of 'ethics' in which questions of desirability have a central place: an understanding that focuses on questions about the ingredients of the good life. It makes sense to ask whether an attachment that is, in whole or in part, the outcome of the use of endomimetic love drugs could authentically count as such an ingredient in just the same way as its naturally produced counterpart almost certainly does.

2 The Core Argument for the Use of Love Drugs

The core argument for the use of (chiefly, endomimetic) love drugs, advanced by Earp, Savulescu, Sandberg, and their colleagues, is a remarkably straightforward and simple one, which can be stated with relative brevity. The bulk of the work the authors have produced on the topic of such drugs, then, involves their elaborating upon and defending that argument's various stages, anticipating objections to it, and responding to the counterarguments of their critics.

The authors' most enduring, prominent, and definite conclusion is that the use of (non-psychedelic) love drugs is morally permissible and desirable. That is, couples have a *moral right* to use love drugs to help deepen or rescue their relationships, should they wish to, but they also have *good reason* to use them. How do the authors reach this twin conclusion?

We can set out their argument as follows:

- There is a three-way clash between (1) our evolved natures; (2) our relationship values and the conditions of our personal happiness; and (3) certain facts about contemporary human life, especially in affluent societies.
- In particular, so far as (1) is concerned, our species evolved, in the Pleistocene epoch, to form pair bonds that would last long enough to ensure the rearing of children. At that distant point in our history, the human life span would have been around twenty to thirty-five years, so there would have been no selection pressure for any great longevity in relationships. The biological machinery underlying our romantic lives and our attachment to partners was 'designed' to sustain what seem to us to be relatively short relationships. In the period in which they first arose, those pair bonds would probably have been 'till death do us part'.
- Turning to (2), we can note that natural selection is concerned only with evolutionary fitness: that is, with our capacity to pass on our genes successfully and ensure our offspring gain the best chance of surviving long enough to do the same. The 'aims' of natural selection, then, are not necessarily in accord with our individual goals. We are each greatly concerned with and place considerable value on our own happiness, and successful relationships are a prime source of such happiness. Quite apart from their instrumental

worth, we very often also value relationships for themselves (as we shall see in Section 5, at least one philosopher thinks that this point does not receive its due emphasis in the authors' work and that it often appears as something of an afterthought). However, where the process of natural selection happens to produce personal well-being or delivers what we value, it does so only as a side effect of features that promote fitness. If we rely on blind evolutionary forces to provide lives that are fulfilling for us, we will likely be disappointed. What is more, dominant social norms concerning relationships stress that marriage ought to be a life-long commitment, and that our relationships ought to be monogamous. But such values, in combination with our evolved natures, are not easily followed, given our contemporary modes of existence.

- This brings us onto (3), the final strut in our discordant situation. Our life expectancy – again, at least in affluent countries – is considerably longer than it was at the time that our romantic neurochemistry evolved. Biologically, it is still as if we were living in the Pleistocene, with a need to sustain relationships for no longer than around fifteen years at most. Thus, our evolved nature is a poor match for current relationship norms – in many cases, attachment will wane simply because the underlying biology is not equipped to maintain it (in their initial paper, Savulescu and Sandberg note that the median duration of those modern marriages that eventually break down is around eleven years, a period to which the fifteen years of a Pleistocene pair bond is 'surprisingly close'[20]). As the authors neatly put it, modern relationships often 'outlast their evolved scaffolding',[21] and, as a result, lose their vibrancy and colour. There are other factors in modern life that put pressure on the ideal of a long-lived, monogamous relationship. For example, the availability of reliable methods of birth control and the potential for far-flung travel (away from the gaze of one's spouse and the prying eyes of one's local community) both present prime opportunities for infidelity, a major cause of relationship breakdown.[22] The headline is this: the neural systems that are responsible for the maintenance of pair bonds are not at home in contemporary affluent society.

- Predictably, the conflict caused by this three-way clash between recalcitrant biology, personal values, and the conditions of contemporary life can have a significant and detrimental effect on our well-being. Until recently, had we wished to avoid that clash, our only choices would have been to modify our values and/or societal norms around marriage and relationships, or to alter the conditions of our existence. The former move would have been extremely difficult or nigh-on impossible, while it is hard to understand that the latter move could have required anything reasonable of us. Should we purposely decrease our life expectancies? Should we permanently root ourselves in small communities, where the possible disapproval of our fellows could act as a deterrent to illicit affairs, and eschew travel? (The authors mention other possible interventions, in the shape of covenant marriages or similar arrangements that significantly raise the costs of divorce, but these seem in many ways undesirable and at any rate somewhat desperate, and possibly ineffectual, measures.[23]) Certainly, deliberately altering our neurochemistry in order to support attachment to our partners has not hitherto been an option.

- However, we now find ourselves with a developing knowledge of the neuro-biological underpinnings of relationships: we have, that is, a growing aware-ness of the nature and action of the hormones, neurotransmitters, and neural pathways implicated in love. To the extent that this body of knowledge grows, so too will our ability to intervene, through the use of so-called love drugs, in the structures of lust, attraction, and attachment that form the basis of our romantic lives. In getting our biology under control in this way, we will be freed from its dominion — in particular, we will be able, at least in some degree, to mould it so that it is a better fit for our values and aspirations and makes a greater contribution to our well-being.

- But would such control be ethically acceptable? Well, plausibly there exists, as a specialized instance of a wider ethical principle of autonomy, a principle of *marital* autonomy, which holds that, other things being equal (so long as no-one is harmed, coerced, and so on), 'Couples in a relationship should have privacy and freedom to form and act on their conception of what a good relationship is for themselves .... People should be free to shape their relationship in the way which best fits them'.[24]

- Therefore (and this is the first part of the authors' conclusion), since other things either are equal or can be made equal through careful regulation and so on, it is morally permissible (on the grounds of the principle of marital autonomy) for couples to attempt to sustain or rescue their rela-tionships through the use of love drugs, if and when such drugs become available.[25]

- Break-ups of relationships bring much suffering and heartache, while being in a loving relationship brings with it well-documented hedonic and health benefits. In addition, as mentioned above, we tend to accord intrinsic value to long-lasting, successful relationships. Relationships of that sort are also consistent with various deeply embedded social norms. There is, then, good reason to maintain and, where appropriate, rescue such relationships.[26]

- Therefore (the second part of the authors' conclusion), given that it is morally permissible to make use of love drugs, there can, in many cases, also be good reason to do so.

That, in essence, is the core argument for the use of non-psychedelic love drugs that we find in the work of Earp, Savulescu, and their co-authors. I have mentioned that its two-part conclusion is the authors' most enduring thesis. In a 2012 paper, Earp, Sandberg, and Savulescu argued for an additional conclusion: that there will be circumstances in which couples are not only permitted but *obliged* to make use of love drugs, provided that all more conventional attempts to save their relationship have been unsuccessful.[27] These are circumstances in which couples have dependent children who would suffer as a result of their parents' divorce. As Pilar Lopez-Cantero points out, Earp and Savulescu, in their 2020 book, appear (without any real fanfare, as is so often the case when – as happens fairly frequently – they change their minds) to have rowed back from this claim.[28] There, they provide a more nuanced account of the various moral and other pressures on parents – and particularly on women, given that 'women are usually expected to do the lion's share of childcare . . . [and thus] . . . "do it for the children"-type arguments tend to have asymmetrical implications for mothers versus fathers, assuming a heterosexual couple'.[29] The weightiest claim they are now prepared to make in this area seems to fall some way short of the suggestion that there can sometimes be a strict duty to use love drugs for the sake of any children who may be negatively affected by their caregivers' divorce. Their current position is that 'the strongest contender for a relationship in which love-enhancing drugs would be in principle justified is a case of this kind'.[30] The only *obligation* to take love drugs they ever recognized has been demoted to an additional item on the list of good reasons to take them.

In ending an account of their core argument, we need to note that our authors are convinced (and increasingly so in their later work) that endomimetic and psychedelic love drugs should only ever be used as an adjunct to traditional relationship therapy.[31] The reasons for this will become apparent as we proceed.

3 The Relationship between Romantic Love and Biology: Avoiding Reductionism

As we have seen, the authors are impressed by our growing knowledge of love's biology and think that it can and should be deployed to help us overcome the three-way clash identified in their core argument. The emerging scientific data that show certain neurochemicals to be involved in the formation and maintenance of our close relationships are clear, even where the details remain a little murky. As I mentioned in my introduction, we need to join the authors in accepting them. There is no longer any mileage at all in holding that romantic love is something wholly 'spiritual' or 'ethereal', with no connection at all to the workings of the brain or the endocrine system. Yet, even when those scientific findings are accepted, philosophers will have questions about the precise relationship between the neurological facts and those higher-level romantic phenomena with which humankind was familiar long before the birth of modern science.

Some of the scientists whose work is cited approvingly by the authors tend towards a somewhat reductionist view of the relation between romance and neurology. Some, for example, imply that love, or its three phases, are 'nothing but' the neurological processes in which oxytocin, vasopressin, dopamine, and so on play a role, adhering to a thoroughgoing reduction of the mental to the neural. Throughout their own work, however, our authors – despite their general enthusiasm for the scientific literature – are chary of subscribing to this or any other form of reductionism about love. In this section, I will detail their adherence to a number of different anti-reductionist stances, as well as setting out another form of anti-reductionism to which they perhaps ought to subscribe, even though they do not appear explicitly to mention it. In short, there is evidence that they oppose the forms of reductionism to which we might give the following labels:

- mental-state/neural-state reductionism
- biological reductionism
- phase reductionism
- isolated-state reductionism.

I want to suggest that it would be sensible for them also to resist something we can call 'cross-image reductionism'.

There can be no doubt that the authors have firm philosophical and/or scientific reasons for rejecting various forms of reductionism. In addition, however, there are certain strategic benefits to their explicitly and decisively *emphasizing* that rejection. Such emphasis allows them, that is, to head off two important concerns that are likely to occur to people as soon as they learn that potentially effective love drugs are on the horizon.

- **Concern 1:** On being told that our growing neurobiological knowledge means we will soon be able to bring our romantic lives under greater control, we might feel that this robs love of some or all of its magic, revealing that it has all along been nothing more than 'a bunch of mindless brain chemicals swirling around in our skulls',[32] which are in principle subject to manipulation at will. That revelation might lead us to think that the aspects of love that we value, or its phenomenology, are in fact illusory, a trick of the light conjured up by the action of neurotransmitters and the firing of certain synapses. Our cherished conception of love might not survive this new understanding: the appearances may well not be saved. As far as our authors are concerned, the rejection of certain forms of romantic reductionism is able to ride to our rescue here – we have no reason to think that biology's being implicated in love entails that love is nothing above and beyond biology.

- **Concern 2:** If love were ultimately reducible to biology, then we would perhaps be led to a worry mentioned in my introduction: that increased power over our biological natures will result in an undesirable, excessive level of control over whom and what we love. As we have already seen, our authors concede that there is a logically possible degree of control over love that it would be undesirable for us to attain. Nevertheless, they are convinced that love drugs will not put such extreme control in our hands. Their assurance here, it seems to me, is again a consequence of their dismissal of certain types of reductionism about love.

I want now to consider in turn each variety of reductionism listed above and show how our authors' rejection of them is supposed to allay the worries expressed in Concerns 1 and 2.

3.1 Mental-State/Neural-State Reductionism

A paradigm example of this first form of reductionism is found in the work of Larry J. Young, a neuroscientist to whom our authors not infrequently appeal when citing research into love's biological underpinnings. In a *Nature* article optimistically entitled 'Love: Neuroscience reveals all', Young writes that 'biologists may soon be able to reduce certain mental states associated with love to a biochemical chain of events'.[33] Despite the rather peculiar suggestion that the biologists themselves will effect the reduction, Young's position here is clear: the mental states (or certain of them, at any rate) associated with love *just are* neural goings-on. This is mental-state/neural-state reductionism in a nutshell. Seemingly with Concerns 1 and 2 in mind, our authors appear to want to reject it, especially in their earlier work. In the event, however, they end up doing so do in a rather tentative, half-hearted way.

In a (perhaps damagingly) short 2014 paper, Savulescu and Earp seem at the outset to be intent on mounting a coherent argument against mental-state/neural-state reductionism, but puzzlingly end up doing nothing of the sort.[34] With a little more commitment, in a 2013 paper, Earp, Wudarczyck, Sandberg, and Savulescu write, 'we do not claim that "love" is *reducible* to brain-states – at least not in any straightforward, non-trivial way'.[35] But there are two things to note here. First, the authors are not in this quotation unambiguously urging that love does *not* reduce to brain states; they are doing no more than distancing themselves from the claim that it *is* thus reducible. Secondly, it is not clear what work the qualification they add to their position is doing or, indeed, precisely what it means. What for example distinguishes A's reducing to B in a trivial way from A's reducing to B in a non-trivial way? Is the implication that love might be reducible to brain states in a *trivial* way? Just what would that involve?

Nonetheless, one thing about which the authors are very definite is our undeniable datum: that brain states are implicated in romantic love. A result of this is that 'brain-level, neurochemical interventions can *affect* feelings of love, in roughly systematic ways'.[36] But this claim does not exactly entail opposition to mental-state/neural-state reductionism. In the final analysis, our authors appear to want to pledge their allegiance to anti-reductionism concerning love and brain states, rather than satisfactorily explain it.

One way in which they often describe the relation of brain states to love might seem to give voice to that under-argued-for allegiance. That is, they frequently talk of neural goings-on as 'underlying' love. If x is said to underlie y, that might suggest that x and y are assumed to be distinct, with y thereby irreducible to x.[37] Yet, as Andrew McGee notes, what *precisely* our authors think the relation of x's underlying y consists in is left frustratingly vague. In other words, while the notion of brain states 'underlying' love is clearly metaphorical, the authors never get around to cashing the metaphor. Thus, as McGee writes, 'there is a real possibility that they have merely paid lip service to anti-[mental-state/neural-state] reductionism by *decreeing* that they do not adopt a reductionist account'.[38]

A response that the authors make to McGee quite badly misses his point. They write:

> The relationship [between brain states and love] is unclear because it depends on one's conception of love – and we have not taken a stand in favor of any single conception to anchor our ethical discussion .... *If* you see 'love' as having X, Y, and Z characteristics, *then* we may be able to sketch out the specific relationship between love – so conceived – and the relevant underlying brain systems and associated interventions. But we need not settle on a specific account of love to argue that there is a relationship between these levels.[39]

McGee's complaint, remember, is that it is unclear what *in general* the relation of x's underlying y comprises. In their response, Earp and Savulescu seem to assume that the general nature of that relation is already understood and all that is not obvious in their writings is how they think it holds between love and neural states in particular. They then go on to give a reason *why* it is not obvious: because they have not committed themselves to any particular conception of love. That this is their approach is evidenced by the fact that they simply help themselves to the notion of *x*'s underlying *y* as part of a response that should really strive to give an account of that relation; they talk, note, of 'the relevant *underlying* brain systems'. The exact nature of the relation of *x*'s underlying *y* remains vague, and no relevant excuse for that vagueness is presented.

Of course, the question of whether or not mental states are to be identified with brain states is an extraordinarily knotty one, and it cannot be adequately dealt with in the sorts of works produced by our authors, which are, after all, like this Element, primarily concerned with ethics rather than with the philosophy of mind. However, in so far as an opposition to mental-state /neural-state reductionism is deployed in our authors' work with the aim of addressing Concern 1, it is questionable whether it needs to be. That is, it might be possible to take a relaxed attitude towards such reductionism, while avoiding the risk of falling into an impoverished view of love or one that regards the valued aspects of love as tantamount to illusion. In other words, the reducibility of love to neural states might not entail the diminishment of love in any way.

One way of achieving this end would be to adopt the sort of view of mind and consciousness to which Galen Strawson subscribes. Strawson advances his view in an article that sets out to dismiss eliminitavism about the mental, where eliminitavism is the view that the mental does not exist. The eliminativist, he thinks, is steered towards her peculiar position – one which he calls 'the silliest claim that has ever been made'[40] – by, ironically, the same sort of considerations that move other philosophers to become mind/brain dualists. That is, the starting point of both eliminativists and dualists is that we know enough about the physical to be able to assert that it could not possibly possess the characteristic features of the mental. So, either the mental is entirely distinct from the physical, constituting a separate ontological category (the dualist stance), or all that exists is physical, and the mental is merely an illusion (the eliminativist stance). But, thinks Strawson, that shared starting point is mistaken. We dupe ourselves if we suppose that we know enough about the physical to be able warrantedly to assert that it could not possess the characteristic features of the mental. That is simply not the case: it is wrong to assume that 'we've got the nature of the physical pretty much taped'.[41] If we are intellectually honest, we are instead compelled to agree with the physicist Arthur Eddington that, when we observe the behaviour of matter, we can ultimately only say '*Something unknown is doing we don't know what*' (italics in original).[42]

The upshot, in Strawson's view, is that there is no reason to suppose that the characteristic features of the mental – consciousness, intentionality, and so on –

are not features of matter. Thus, Strawson is perfectly happy to say that the mental reduces to the physical, so long as the notion of reduction is not thought to connote any sort of diminishment. If you like, mind is not downgraded to inert, lumpen matter in Strawson's naturalistic metaphysic; rather, what we previously thought of as blind, inert matter is upgraded to encompass the majesty of mind.

Understandably, a proper assessment of Strawson's position would require much more space than I have available. I will have to rest content, then, with a conditional claim: *if* Strawson's position is a compelling one, there is no requirement for our authors to eschew mental-state/neural-state reductionism in order to evade Concern 1. But what if we are unconvinced by Strawson's arguments? Will our authors still owe us a persuasive defence of their stance? I do not think so. This is because, over the course of their writings, they quietly abandon their opposition to mental-state/neural-state reductionism, chiefly in favour of a dismissal of what I shall call biological reductionism.

3.2 Biological Reductionism

In the authors' later work, and chiefly in their 2020 book, the *direct* question of the reducibility of love specifically to the neural is sidestepped, and a distinct, much clearer, and more fully explained form of anti-reductionism introduced. Here, love is not reducible to the biological (and so by implication – though this is not their central focus – to the neural), because love is a phenomenon with a dual nature. It is both biological and, as they put it, 'psychosocial'.

This position is heavily influenced by the work of Carrie Jenkins. In her book *What Love Is*, Jenkins argues that, while the work of neurobiologists has clearly shown love to be at least in part biological, this cannot be the whole story. There is a considerable element of social construction at work in romantic love, which is missed if we regard it as an unalloyed biological phenomenon: 'A purely biological theory predicts that cultural influences play a negligible to nonexistent role in determining the nature of romantic love. Our biology is not in any substantial way a product of society or culture. So, if love is part of our biology, love is not in any substantial way a product of society or culture'.[43] According to Jenkins, however, this only demonstrates the inadequacy of a purely biological theory of romantic love. Just as much as it is (nowadays) a given that neurochemistry is involved in romantic love, it is also undeniable that what sort of love *counts* as romantic is subject to temporal and cultural variation. What we now, in Western societies, categorize as romantic love – with, perhaps, a strong emphasis on sexual desire and sexual activity – would not have been so regarded in Victorian England. This is something rather more substantial than, and importantly different from, the claim that romantic love finds different expressions across time and place. Jenkins's thought – in common with those who maintain, unlike her, that love is exclusively a social construct – is rather that what romantic love *is* in one time or place is not necessarily what romantic love is at another time or place.

Now, that variation in the very nature of romantic love, Jenkins argues, is inexplicable if the phenomenon is exclusively biological:

> Ancient, evolved brain chemistry and fundamental human drives don't differ radically among cultures and don't change much in the space of a few hundred years. So why does romantic love seem to vary so much across time and across cultures if it is a biological phenomenon? This is the one big question to which a simple biological theory of love cannot give any answer that I would find satisfying. The theory predicts some individual variation in different people's cocktail recipes for love, but biology alone cannot adequately explain these large-scale variations that look like they are tracking cultural differences.[44]

So, romantic love has a dual nature: it is, in Jenkins's way of expressing the point, both biological and social. The human biological actor gets to play different roles – roles that may or may not fall within the realm of romantic love, depending on cultural circumstances – with different social scripts that are particular to time and place.

As I have said, this dual-nature account comes to be adopted by our authors and constitutes their central, or what we might call their considered, anti-reductionism. A boon for them is that it interlaces nicely with one of the essential features of their core argument – the possible conflict between our evolved biological natures and the network of social scripts and inculcated norms and values within which we operate. It may be that certain social scripts – ones involving extremely long-lasting, monogamous commitments – are a poor fit for the capacities of the biological actor. If they are, then one option that looks increasingly possible (albeit an option to which, as it happens, Jenkins would not want to sign up[45]) is pharmaceutically to 'upgrade' our biology in such a way that it harmonizes with the script.

A further advantage of our authors' rejection of biological reductionism, and their embracing of the dual-nature account, is that it arguably allows them to lay Concern 1 to rest and go at least some way towards addressing Concern 2. If love is both biological *and* social, then love cannot simply be identified with the action of a set of chemicals, regardless of whether or not the mental reduces to the neural. And even if endomimetic love drugs were to give us complete control over the biological aspects of love, the social aspects would lie beyond their influence. It may be thought that this still raises the spectre of a possible excess of control over our romantic lives. After all, *too much* control may theoretically exist in the absence of *total* control. However, it seems to me that our authors think that that troubling phantom can be decisively laid to rest by their opposition to two other forms of romantic reductionism: phase reductionism and isolated-state reductionism.

3.3 Phase Reductionism

By the expression 'phase reductionism', I mean to indicate the view that love is reducible to its phases – lust, attraction, and attachment – either individually or in combination. It appears that one prominent adherent to phase reductionism is Helen Fisher, who writes as if lust, attraction, and attachment exhaust love (this, it appears, is what allows her confidently to declare that animals love[46] – they are subject to these three forces). On this issue, despite her considerable influence on their scientific understanding of love, our authors part company with Fisher. They write, for example, that: 'Biological interventions can ... produce the phases of the evolution of a loving relationship: lust, attraction and attachment. They can increase the probability of a loving relationship occurring, but they cannot by themselves cause love.'[47] So, since it is possible for lust, attraction, and attachment to be 'produced' without love thereby being brought into being, love is not reducible to lust, attraction, or attachment, or to any combination thereof. (It is worth noting in passing that the authors appear in this quotation to be aligning themselves with what, in Section 4, I will call the 'productive approach' to the action of love drugs.)

Here, I want to side with our authors over Fisher. First of all, it would seem that lust is at best a precursor to love (and an unnecessary one at that – asexual people engage in romantic relationships), rather than a stage or component of it. Secondly, it is commonly held that we may be attracted or even romantically attached to another with whom we are merely infatuated. Love seems to be – and is usually taken to be – something more than infatuation and, therefore, necessarily more than either attraction or attachment. What more it is, precisely, is an issue I will come back to in Section 6.

It should be easy to see how the rejection of phase reductionism might be thought to address Concern 2, though whether it *genuinely* does so is a question to which we will return in Section 4. That is, even if the use of love drugs were guaranteed to produce lust, attraction, and attachment, it would not thereby be guaranteed to cause love. An excessive level of control over the phenomenon of love would thus be avoided.

3.4 Isolated-State Reductionism

The denial that love drugs would deliver an excessive level of control over our romantic lives might seem to be supported by the rejection of what we might call 'isolated-state reductionism' (though the question of whether it is or not will return for us later). The mistake of such reductionism, even given a general mental-state/neural-state reductionism of the sort to which Young appears to subscribe, is to suppose that, for example, the activity of oxytocin is individually sufficient for the formation of a pair bond or for the maintenance of an existing attachment. Biologists are eager to point out that this is not the case: a number of hormones will be expressed in any behaviour, and a neurochemical only ever functions to produce a characteristic effect against a complex background of enabling conditions. That characteristic effect can, therefore, be defeated by the absence of any of those conditions. To say that oxytocin produces or maintains attachment is properly understood as a sort of shorthand for saying that it is a key trigger in such production or maintenance. The drawing of a parallel might shed light here: while it is quite correct to say that the striking of a match results in a flame, it can be taken as read that it does so only in the presence of background conditions such as the existence of oxygen in the atmosphere.

Helen Fisher, for example, in discussing the conclusion that dopamine and/or norepinephrine are implicated in attraction between animals, has this to say: 'More brain chemicals are undoubtedly involved . . . . A lot of chemical systems undoubtedly coordinate in some sort of chain reaction to trigger feelings of animal attraction.'[48] And, as Earp and Savulescu note in their 2020 book, the endocrinologist Kim Wallen writes: 'Hormones are not absolute regulators of behavior. The function of hormones is to shift that balance of behavior in one direction or another. The presence of certain hormones doesn't mean you will exhibit a certain behavior but rather increases the probability that you might.'[49] This point perhaps helps us to see why our authors are unconcerned about love drugs delivering too much power into our hands. The power we will have once love drugs are available is simply that of self-administering certain substances. To do that is not to guarantee that our attachment to another will be strengthened; it is merely to increase the probability of deepened or rejuvenated attachment. A whole orchestra of other conditions, most of which will be (currently) beyond our control, will need to harmonize with our taking the drug before, so to speak, any romantic airs can be played.

We might distinguish pithily between the rejection of phase reductionism and the rejection of isolated-state reductionism by saying this: where anti-phase reductionism tells us that, say, attachment can exist in the absence of love, anti-isolated-state reductionism tells us that oxytocin can be at work in our nervous systems in the absence of attachment.

3.5 Cross-Image Reductionism

The rejection of isolated-state reductionism means that, even assuming mental-state/neural-state reductionism (so, even if all mental states are – possibly quite complex – physical states), it is impossible to point to some one bit of (say) neural activity and accurately say something like 'There is some romantic attachment'. It seems to me that the best we could say, perhaps on viewing an fMRI scan of a brain, would be something like 'This is what the brain of a romantically attached person looks like.' But note how that claim is worded. It would be peculiar, and I think inaccurate, to say instead 'This is what a brain that is romantically attached looks like.' According to our quotidian understanding of love – which, recall, we are trying to keep in view throughout, as the thing that really matters to us and our reason for considering the likely efficacy and desirability of love drugs in the first place – it is *persons* who are attracted to other persons, who are attached to other persons, and who love other persons. Certainly, we are admitting that they do so *in virtue* of what is going on at the neural level, but that does not mean that it is their neurology that is attracted, attached, or in love. As a comparison, consider an example from Michael Dummett, used admittedly in a wholly different context. From the fact that an athlete wins a medal in virtue of her speed, it does not follow that it was the speed that won the medal.[50]

To suggest that it is our brains or our neurochemistry that are the subjects of attachment or love does violence to the concepts of attachment or love with which we are familiar, and in which we are interested. This is not always appreciated by neuroscientists. Consider some of Young's language in his *Nature* article: love, he writes, is 'an emergent property of a cocktail of ancient neuropeptides and neurotransmitters'.[51] Insofar as we can accurately describe love as a property at all, it seems that it must be a property of persons, rather than of a collection of neurochemicals. The ascription of love properly occurs at the person-level, rather than at the neural level. It is worth noting in this connection that Fisher too veers away from our ordinary conception of love, in entitling a TED talk 'The brain in love'.[52] Brains do not fall in love. Persons with brains do, even though they doubtless do so in virtue of what is going on in their brains.

To help us appreciate this point, we can appeal to a rather loose version of Wilfrid Sellars's distinction between the scientific image and the manifest image of what he calls 'man-in-the-world', which we might update to 'human-kind-in-the-world'.[53] Our experience of love, and the experiential knowledge we have had of that phenomenon since a time long before we even knew of the existence of oxytocin, vasopressin, and the rest, are part of the manifest image. And the fundamental objects in that image or framework are *persons*. Not so in the scientific image: here we encounter objects, substances, and properties that exist at a much finer level of discrimination.

Very roughly speaking, we could portray the manifest image as what Sophie Grace Chappell calls 'the *War and Peace* world', while the scientific image is (again, somewhat crudely) what she calls the 'atoms-and-the-void' world.[54] Whereas the latter world (or, perhaps better, the latter way of *understanding* the world) is basically that of Democritus or of modern physics, the former is the one composed of persons with motives, emotions, insecurities, and so on: 'a world of lovers and battles, romantic hopes and unromantic doubts, pecuniary cares and political fears, rapture and *ennui*, taciturn rationalist fathers and fulsome fideist sons, partings in drunkenness and reunions in sobriety, social pride and the peasant's pride in a good scythe-action, the *beau monde* and the *demi-monde*, the emperor and the nursery girl.'[55] While Chappell wants to accord ontological priority to the *War and Peace* world, regarding the world of atoms and the void as essentially an abstraction from it, Sellars, if anything, wants to reverse that order of priority, although he does tell us that the scientific image is necessarily formulated from within the manifest image.[56] Nonetheless, there is no suggestion that the manifest image is unreal or that it somehow gets things wrong, even though the ultimate explanation of the nature of things is to be found in the scientific image. This is just as well: the aspect under which attachment and attraction interest us, and seem worth pursuing or strengthening, is that of the manifest image. We would have no interest at all in these phenomena were they *merely* the sorts of brain activity that show up on fMRI scans – our real concern with them lies wholly at the level of persons and with the effects that they might have on that level of humankind-in-the-world.

With these thoughts in mind, it should be clear why I call the form of reductionism I am warning against 'cross-image reductionism'. What Young and Fisher are guilty of in the examples given is a heedless mixing of elements from two distinct frameworks: distinct despite their conceptualizing the same reality. Under their way of presenting things, it is not primarily persons who are in love. It is mélanges of neurotransmitters and neuropeptides, or brains. Again, it would be foolish, given the scientific data, to deny that neurochemicals and brains are implicated in love, attraction, attachment, and so on. But the only objects of which love, attraction, and attachment can properly be predicated are persons. To suggest otherwise is to be guilty of a confusion of images and the transposition of elements of one framework to another in which they are not at home.

Although I suggest that our authors should oppose cross-image reductionism, a possible tension might be detected between such opposition on the one hand, and the Jenkins-inspired dual-nature account of love to which they subscribe on the other. That is, all talk of the biological correlates of love might seem to belong exclusively to the scientific image, and all talk of love proper – since love is predicated of and centred on persons – to the manifest image. If that is the case, and if cross-image reductionism is false, then it would appear inaccurate to say, as Jenkins and our authors do, that biological factors form a part or aspect of love. Rather, we should say merely that love exists *in virtue of* the obtaining of certain biological facts, but that those facts, since they belong to the subpersonal realm captured by the scientific image, cannot legitimately be represented as a part of love. Given their investment in the dual-nature theory, then, our authors may wish to reject opposition to cross-image reductionism. Whether that move is either necessary or wise is a further question.

4 The Influence of Endomimetic Love Drugs: The Productive Account and the Facilitative Account

I have suggested that the rejection of certain forms of reductionism can help our authors sidestep Concern 2: the worry that the use of love drugs would give us an undesirable and excessive degree of control over romantic phenomena. So, for example, the falsity of phase reductionism means that, even if love drugs are able to produce lust, attraction, or attachment (or any combination thereof), they cannot thereby produce love. Further, the falsity of isolated-state reductionism entails that even lust, attraction, and attachment cannot be automatically brought into existence by a subject's imbibing a love drug. The production of any of these phases can occur only with the co-operation of a host of enabling conditions.

I suspect it is their wholly warranted dismissal of isolated-state reductionism that allows Savulescu and others to be at ease in echoing the language of control, production, regulation, and modulation, which often occurs in the scientific literature's discussion of the action of oxytocin and other neurochemicals, and which I have myself used so far in this Element. So, our authors occasionally describe patterns of lust, attraction, and attachment as being *regulated* by neurochemistry. For example, in their initial paper, they write that parent–child and partner–partner bonds 'have the same physiological *regulation*'.[57] In a 2015 paper, they state that '[b]rain chemicals such as oxytocin, dopamine, testosterone, and many others seem to *regulate* our interpersonal drives and emotions, including the formation of romantic pair-bonds'.[58] This, as I have said, simply mirrors some of the language used in the scientific literature; one of the papers cited by Savulescu and Sandberg has the title 'Nucleus accumbens oxytocin and dopamine interact to *regulate* pair bond formation in female prairie voles.'[59] On other occasions, our authors talk instead of modulation, writing that the 'different love-related systems [lust, attraction, and attachment] can be *modulated* by chemical stimuli',[60] and: 'Drugs affecting particular brain systems at particular times would enable more fine-tuned marital therapy but possibly also *modulation* of the strength of pair bonding, mate selection and levels of sexual (or emotional) desire.'[61] Since they offer no special account of how their use of the terms 'regulate/regulation' and 'modulate/modulation' is to be understood, we are driven to assume that they are employed in something like their ordinary sense. The *Oxford English Dictionary (OED)* lists various senses for the verb 'regulate', the common element in which is the notion of control: if x regulates y, then x controls y. So, for example, the degree to which the accelerator is depressed in a car regulates or controls the speed at which the car moves. Whenever the accelerator is depressed, the car speeds up. And, other things being equal, the depression of the accelerator is sufficient for the car's speed increasing. At least in its non-musical senses, the word 'modulate' would appear to be a near-synonym of 'regulate' and to be definable in terms of it. Thus, one sense listed in the *OED* is 'To exert a modifying or controlling influence on; to *regulate*'.

My point is this. The authors can happily talk of control or production of romantic phenomena – and so can subscribe to what we might call a *productive account* of the action of love drugs – given the understanding that such control or production only ever occurs when a range of other things (enabling conditions) are equal. For example, while oxytocin is necessary for attachment, it is sufficient only in combination with an array of other factors. And that means, our authors seem to think, that we need have no concerns that the control love drugs would give us would ever be excessive. Taking a drug intended to strengthen or deepen attachment can only increase the probability that that goal will be achieved. Much is still left to chance. We need not fear that the productive account entails the sort of intuitively undesirable situation described by Jenkins: 'Perhaps one day we'll be able to manipulate human pair-bonding . . . . Perhaps we'll bring falling in and out of love under total control, rendering it as simple as opening and closing an app on our smartphones.'[62] Even so, we can, I think, sensibly question our authors' confidence that Concern 2 has been altogether evaded with the rejection of (in particular) isolated-state reductionism. Let us imagine a situation in which, luckily, all the enabling conditions that will allow a dose of oxytocin to do its intended work are in place. What guarantees that the degree of control we *then* have – when the drug actually does its work – is not excessive? It does not seem to help to say, 'Well, it was unlikely to work, so the control is not particularly substantial.' It *has* worked. Control has, against the odds, been achieved. And there seems no reason to think that that control could not be substantial or even excessive.

Consider a parallel case. Suppose a bank of 100 switches, only one of which, when flipped, will turn on a light bulb. You are granted just one attempt at selecting the correct switch. Against the odds, you choose it, and the light bulb is illuminated. That you were statistically unlikely to pick the 'live' switch has no impact at all on the degree of control you have over the light bulb's illumination once you have flipped that particular switch.

Fortunately, however, there is an alternative account of the action of substances like oxytocin to be found in the scientific literature. This account, which we can call the *facilitative account*, is also frequently deployed by our authors, in addition to (though never explicitly contrasted with) their talk of regulation and modulation. The thought behind the account is that the action of love drugs is purely facilitative, rather than productive. To be more precise: instead of producing, say, attachment, a love drug would produce some other factor F, where F is such as to provide fertile ground for the development or growth of attachment, but not such as to cause attachment. F would facilitate attachment, but not compel it; it would *allow* it to grow, or provide an environment favourable to its development, but would not lead directly to it. Our authors mention three candidates for F, one of which is improved interpersonal communication. (Since there are experimental data supporting each candidate, it is most likely the case that oxytocin produces all three, even if it does not invariably produce them together.)

4.1 Factor F As Improved Communication

The authors' developed position, it will be recalled, is that love drugs aimed at rekindling attachment should only ever be used as an adjunct to relationship therapy. This claim seems in part to be based upon experimental findings concerning the administration of exogenous oxytocin:

> [A] seminal study ... showed that oxytocin can facilitate positive communication – and reduce stress levels – in romantic couples engaged in an argument. In this double-blind, placebo-controlled study, heterosexual couples received oxytocin (versus placebo) before engaging in a conversation about a chronic source of conflict .... Oxytocin increased the ratio of positive to negative communication behaviors and facilitated a more rapid reduction in cortisol levels after the conflict. Importantly, couples' therapy – when it *is* effective – is believed to work best by enhancing partners' communication skills; and ... the ratio of positive to negative communication behaviors is strongly predictive of long-term relationship survival.[63]

Were these sorts of results only available for 'romantic couples', we could legitimately proffer an interpretation of the action of exogenous oxytocin that differs markedly from the intended one. That is, while the findings here are consistent with oxytocin's producing positive communication behaviours, which then make deepened or sustained romantic attachment possible, they are also consistent with an 'attachment-first' interpretation, according to which oxytocin directly strengthens romantic attachment as per the productive account, which in turn facilitates improved communication.

However, it seems wider data indicate that exogenously administered oxytocin improves communication in contexts other than the romantic.[64] The thought, then, is that the action of oxytocin is a sufficient (though perhaps not necessary) condition of good communication, while good communication is a necessary though not sufficient condition of deepening, strengthening, or maintaining romantic attachment. It can thus be used to increase the chances of relationship therapy bearing fruit, which explains our authors' insistence that such love drugs should only be used in concert with such therapy.

While this undoubtedly helps us to swerve Concern 2, it might lead us to wonder why oxytocin is billed as, specifically, a love drug, rather than as simply a communication-improving drug. Good communication can, happily, exist between individuals – colleagues, say, or friends, or heads of state – without there being the slightest possibility of a romantic attachment forming. And a series of relationship therapy sessions in which communication is open, honest, and non-aggressive may still result in a couple recognizing that they have no reason to stay together. That is most likely as it should be, but it still leaves room for puzzlement about why oxytocin is touted as a love drug or an attachment enhancer.

4.2 Factor *F* As a 'Pro-Relationship Mindset'

Another candidate for *F* – the state produced by oxytocin that facilitates but does not produce attachment – is what our authors call a 'pro-relationship mindset'.[65] They write:

> Oxytocin administration holds promise for acting in areas that are central to relationship health and functioning. Specifically, oxytocin has been shown to reduce anxiety and stress; boost trust, eye-contact, mind-reading, and empathy; heighten the availability of positive relationship memories; and improve social attention, recognition, and appraisals, as well as the encoding and retrieval of memories with social content. In a relationship context, these effects could (1) increase partner approachability and co-operativeness, (2) increase mutual understanding and perspective-taking, thereby enhancing

learning in the therapeutic process, and (3) increase positive relationship reflections, which are likely to be associated with successful therapy outcomes.[66]

This all sounds unremittingly positive and, again, undoubtedly avoids Concern 2. Oxytocin administration produces the sorts of states listed, all of which are no more than fertile ground for the strengthening or revivification of romantic attachment; it does not, however (according to the facilitative account), produce romantic attachment, even indirectly.

It seems to me that, if this is how oxytocin administration works, there is still room to worry about its effects, and to wonder whether they are altogether desirable. The concern is this. It seems that if the subject of oxytocin administration is made more trusting, less anxious, more approachable, and so on, than she normally is or otherwise would have been, then she herself has been altered in ways that may (though need not necessarily) have an impact on the authenticity of her attachment and any love that is built upon it. In particular, it seems that if I am made more trusting, approachable, co-operative, and so on, then new *reasons* for attachment to my partner might present themselves to me. We may think that this is all well and good, and certainly does not raise the spectre of excessive control over romantic phenomena. After all, reasons, whether newly encountered or not, do not *compel* actions or attitudes, so Concern 2 is not an issue here.

While that is true, my worry is that the subject may still, so to speak, be compelled to have, or be strong-armed into, these reasons by the action of the drug. They may, in a way to be substantially expanded upon in Section 6, not really be her own reasons. After all, something that is for a very trusting person a reason for attachment to another, may not be for a person who is less trusting. If the less trusting person, as it were, pharmaceutically transforms herself into a person of the former sort, she may end up motivated by reasons that are not authentically her own. Again, I will have more to say about why that would be a problem in my Section 6, when I introduce what I call the 'dual-particularity requirement'. The central thought will be that in changing my mindset, and thus my reasons, I potentially undermine the authenticity of any love that may be built on a strengthened attachment, since any authentic love I have must involve attachment grounded in reasons that are authentically my own.

It is important to note that I have buffered these claims with a number of qualifications. I have said that I *may* be strong-armed into seeing certain considerations as reasons; that those reasons *may* not be my own; and that my mindset's being changed would *potentially* render any resulting love inauthentic. The qualifications are necessary because, as I will explain further in Section 6, there are two possible outcomes of my pharmaceutically altering my mindset, so far as reasons for attachment are concerned. It *could* be that the change of mindset allows me accurately to see that some feature of another person, say, has always been a reason for me to be attached to them. If this is how oxytocin works, then its action is 'ground-clearing', much as I held SSRI use may be in my introduction. It removes an impediment to a relationship, in the shape of a blindness to certain reasons that I genuinely have. However, this might not be how oxytocin works. It may instead make me encounter as reasons certain considerations that are in fact not reasons for me (though they may well be for somebody else), given my preferences, constitution, values, and so on. Or, alternatively, it might make these considerations into genuine reasons for me, but only by changing who I am: by changing my preferences, constitution, values, and so on.

4.3 Factor *F* As Enhanced Processing of Bonding Cues

Similar points can be made about our authors' final candidate for *F*, according to which the facilitative factor produced by oxytocin use would be the enhanced processing of bonding cues.[67] They quote a paper by Nadine Striepens and colleagues to explain this notion: 'By acting as a neuroplasticity agent, OXT [that is, oxytocin] may help rewire neural systems, so that specific cues from individuals which [*sic*] whom bonds are formed are more likely to elicit recognition and pleasure in the future.'[68] The authors explain that such cues, or positive social stimuli, would come to be seen as 'salient' by a subject of oxytocin administration. That might seem to suggest that the subject, as a result of the drug's action, would come to see the stimuli as *reasons*, either for attachment or for some other form of romantic engagement or behaviour. And this raises the same concerns as those expressed in Section 4.2, though perhaps even more acutely, given the talk of 'rewiring' neural systems (Striepens and others hold that the effects of therapeutic oxytocin will likely be long-lasting). Again, those concerns will be addressed in detail in Section 6.

4.4 The Productive and Facilitative Accounts, and Concerns 1 and 2

It will be helpful at this point to summarize some of the findings of Sections 3 and 4. Both a productive and a facilitative account of the action of love drugs are detectable in the scientific literature and in the writings of our authors. It may seem that, given the falsity of phase reductionism and, in particular, isolated-state reductionism, the authors can endorse the productive account while evading Concern 2. We have seen, however, that this is not necessarily the case: while on the productive account there is a fair degree of probability that a dose or doses of oxytocin will not produce attachment, when conditions align so that it does, the degree of control placed into the hands of the taker could still be excessive.

A high degree of control over attachment is almost certainly avoided if the facilitative account of oxytocin's action is the correct one. Although Concern 2 will be sidestepped here, it could be that an excessive level of control over attachment is not really what we need to worry about. That is because there is a possibility that oxytocin use will still deliver an undesirable *sort* of control, insofar as it may strong-arm the drug user into having reasons that, while they will not compel attachment, are not really her own. What is more, insofar as the user of exogenous oxytocin comes to see herself – including her reasons for attachment – as something that is essentially chemically manipulable, she may be in danger of evoking Concern 1 and failing to save the appearances of romantic phenomena. Once more, these issues will be further explored in Section 6. What will also emerge there is that we can afford to be agnostic on the question of whether it is the productive or the facilitative account that is correct. This is because, either way, there is some reason to think that the use of endomimetic love drugs would be undesirable.

Before ending this section, there is a further point about the facilitative account that it is worth making. What the facilitative account of course holds is that when romantic attachment does follow, or end up strengthened by one or other candidate (or combination of candidates) for factor F, that attachment is something distinct from the factor that enabled it. Assuming every mental state to have a neural correlate or set of neural correlates, so too will romantic attachment. Presumably, if we could identify that correlate or set of correlates, we could, pharmaceutically or otherwise, induce it – and thus develop or strengthen romantic attachment – directly, and, in the process, threaten the claim about acceptable levels of control that the facilitative account is held to safeguard. Naturally, if such control were thought to be problematic, we could refrain from achieving it, relying instead on merely facilitative therapies like oxytocin. Choosing a less effective over a more effective therapy might seem like an odd choice to make, however, if our aim is to get a relationship back on track.

5 The Object of Love and the Object of the Use of Love Drugs

I want to start this part of our investigation by asking whether there is some sort of dissonance between what a person in a loving relationship finds of value and what is valued by a person who seeks (presumably – or at least ideally – not unilaterally) to help renew a flagging relationship using chemical means.

My conclusion is that, depending on the precise nature of the situation, there may well be a clash between these two things. However, depending on circumstances there *need* not be.

In a landmark paper on the desirability of love drugs, Sven Nyholm asks what it is that we value about love, and, indeed, *how* we value it (that is, whether we take love's value to be intrinsic or merely instrumental).[69] I will have cause later to examine Nyholm's arguments at closer quarters, but for now I want simply to focus on what might at first sight appear to be a curious feature of his approach. That is, he restricts his attention almost entirely to the value that love has *for the beloved*, saying next to nothing about its value to the lover. While this may appear to be an oversight, I think that it in fact gestures towards a significant point, and one that casts at least some doubt on the wisdom of taking drugs to help repair relationships.

Let us imagine a securely attached couple, Jane and Jill, who are in a healthy, non-abusive, mutually endorsed monogamous long-term relationship. (I make mention of a monogamous relationship just because it delivers a manageably simple example; I do not wish to imply that a monogamous relationship is somehow more desirable or healthy than a polyamorous relationship endorsed by all those who participate in it.) Each partner fulfils two roles in the relationship: she is both lover and beloved. *Qua* beloved, Jane values the love she receives from Jill – she values the fact that Jill loves her for who she is, with all her faults, will always be there for her, and so on. The same will of course be true, *mutatis mutandis*, when it comes to what Jill *qua* beloved values. Plausibly, Jane places an intrinsic value on the state of affairs of her receiving Jill's love, even though she may also value the benefits to which it leads. But what does Jane *qua* lover value? Is it once again primarily love, but this time the love that *she* gives, or perhaps her being in the state of loving Jill?

It seems to me that it is neither. Being romantically attached to her beloved means that what she primarily values is not her love for Jill, but the object of that love: *Jill herself.* Derivatively, Jane – since this is *ex hypothesi* a healthy, non-abusive relationship – values her relationship with Jill, because standing in that relationship to her beloved allows her to be close to, benefit, and care for this person whom she values.[70] Does she also value her love for Jill? Plausibly she does, but this is necessarily again a derivative, second-order valuing, parasitic on her valuing Jill. Her loving Jill is her valuing Jill in a particular way, so her valuing her love for Jill is her valuing the fact that she values Jill in that way. She may also, as we will see in more detail shortly, value love generally: she may, and probably will, regard it as valuable that people in general, and she herself, can value others in the way that she values Jill. But this whole cascade of valuing starts with, and gains its impetus from, her valuing Jill in ways that are distinctive of romantic love.

Now, suppose another couple, John and Jim, who once enjoyed the sort of secure relationship that Jane and Jill have, but whose attachment to each other has faded. Perhaps *qua* sadly *ex*-beloved, each misses the love he received from the other. However, *qua* ex-lover John, for example, now no longer values Jim in ways distinctive of romantic love. And yet he misses valuing Jim in that way, perhaps in part because he has, through his experience of having loved Jim, come to value love in general. He values the state of his being in love, even though he no longer values Jim in ways distinctive of romantic love. Jim reveals in discussion that he feels the same way, *mutatis mutandis*.

In an attempt to propel themselves back into a state they each value – the state of being in a loving relationship – John and Jim agree to try love drugs. Is there not something peculiar about what they are aiming at here: about the *object* of their action? That is, the object of their action in taking love drugs is not the same as the object of their now-faded love. The object (in the sense of 'focus') of John's love was Jim, while the object of Jim's love was John. But the object (in the sense of 'goal') of John's taking love drugs is John's achieving a psychological state that he values; the object of Jim's taking love drugs is Jim's achieving a psychological state that *he* values. We might detect here a sort of self-concern on the part of each that was absent from their erstwhile love. When they shared a loving relationship, the primary love-related concern of each was the other – neither was primarily concerned to be in the state of being in love. Insofar as they had an interest in being in that state at all, that interest was simply a consequence of their *already* being in the state, and so of their having each other as their primary focus.

The point here is this. Once the attachment that forms part of human love becomes pharmaceutically manipulable, it becomes possible to aim at that attachment (and ultimately at love) as a desired state: a state that I would like to be in. Where, before such manipulation was feasible, the focus of my attention in being attached was the object of my attachment, that focus now shifts to my being in the state of attachment. But if that is the case, my attention now rests on, and my motivation is guided by, the wrong object.

David Ferraro perhaps has this sort of problem in mind when he characterizes the project of using drugs to control (in some measure) love and attachment as fundamentally narcissistic.[71] It is almost certainly what he means when he identifies as an error the tendency of pro-love-drug writers to use 'love' exclusively as a noun rather than a verb:

> On the one hand, if love is a noun, a thing, this will tend to situate it within (rather than between) individuals. It becomes affective and, ultimately, individualistic, a matter of how one feels . . . .. Love, in this conception of it, is

a strictly private affair . . .. On the other hand, when love is understood as
a verb, it becomes relational – an act, a process between interstices, or, to use
Roland Barthes's term, a 'discourse'.[72]

The idea that 'love' is correctly viewed as a verb rather than a noun is familiar
from the writings of bell hooks.[73] Ferraro's thought in making use of it would
appear to be this: if we regard 'love' primarily as a noun, then we conceptualize
its referent as first and foremost a (desirable) state that individuals can be in,
whereas if we regard it as a (transitive) verb, we think of love as an engaged
activity that essentially has, and is trained upon, an object – as at its heart
a certain sort of orientation towards a part of the world that is wholly independent of the lover. Grasping love in the former manner fails to save the appearances; thinking of it in the latter way leaves the appearances intact.

There are others who would appear to share the sort of worry that Ferraro
voices. Michael Hauskeller, for example, has something similar in mind when
he makes the following comment:

> Understanding the neurophysiology of love is one thing. Seeking to manipu-
> late it is quite another. Love, as it is, takes us beyond ourselves. When we love
> we stop caring about what is good for us. Therein lies the beauty of love. Once
> we have learned to control it, love will be firmly tied to self-interest, and then
> *that* beauty will be gone.[74]

The peculiar beauty of John's love for Jim – a beauty still possessed by Jane's
ongoing love for Jill – lay in, as it were, its *self-forgetting nature*. John first, and
primarily, valued Jim in a way distinctive of romantic love, and only subsequently came to value his valuing Jim in that way, and then to value love in
general. That is, he came to see that there is worth and beauty in someone's
valuing other people in the non-self-interested ways distinctive of romantic
love, where thought about one's own good takes a back seat. He is now – having
recognized its value – aiming directly at that state, but his aiming at it is
motivated by self-interest. He wants to find himself in that desirable state
again, and the goal of achieving it is uppermost in his mind. But the state,
when it originally existed, lacked, so to speak, that kind of focus on itself. It was
a state that wrested John's attention away from himself and his own mental
states, and placed it firmly on Jim.

We might draw a parallel here between virtue and romantic love. According
to virtue ethicists, a virtuous life – a life in which one possesses and exercises
the virtues – is a flourishing life, a life of supreme value to its subject.[75] And yet
a danger looms once this fact (assuming it to be a fact) has been recognized by
an agent. That is, being desirous of flourishing, she may attempt to be virtuous
solely in order to reap the benefits of virtue. But the attempt is bound to fail – to

engage in the sorts of behaviour that virtuous people display, but with the sole aim of benefiting oneself, is not authentically to be virtuous.[76] Here, the object of one's attempt to become virtuous is at odds with the objects of virtue; self-interest crashes headlong into the sort of other-directedness that characterizes the bulk of the virtues. Similarly, John's object in taking love drugs (to find himself in a certain desirable state) is at odds with the essentially other-directed focus of love; it pulls in the opposite direction.

Another parallel might be drawn with an agent's being in a state of concentration on something, call it x. In order authentically to be in this state, you must allow your whole attention to be absorbed by x. If, instead of doing this, you concentrate on getting into the state of concentrating on x, you are unlikely to achieve that state. Concentration and virtue share a certain feature: while both are states *of* an agent, they are at root states that *look away* from themselves, essentially involving a captivation by something else. The same can be said of love.

As already acknowledged, once we have experienced the sort of other-directedness involved in romantic love, we can come to recognize that being in that self-forgetful state is something that is of significant value to human beings, and, as Hauskeller reminds us, possessed of its own particular beauty. This is noted, too, by Susan Wolf, who declares that love is the most important thing in human life, precisely because – regardless of whether it is romantic or familial love, or the love involved in friendship – it 'roots us, motivationally, to the world'.[77] That is, it gives us a source of motivation outside ourselves, breaking (at least insofar as our relationship to our beloved is concerned) the bonds of self-interest. But it is precisely because this is what love does that a tension is created if we find ourselves in John's position, aiming at the state purely because it is a state that we would like ourselves to be in.

Faced with this line of argument, we are apt to think, not inappropriately, that something must have gone awry. The suggestion, that is, seems to be that we ought not to work at cultivating and sustaining love, because to do so would be to undercut the phenomenon we are trying to preserve, foster, or reinstate, by disrupting the characteristic direction of its focus. And that might seem an intolerable and counter-intuitive result. It is, after all, a commonplace that love is something that *needs* to be tended and worked at, and we typically take it as commendable if someone conscientiously engages in such a task, and contemptible if he instead allows his relationships to go to seed. Our authors would agree, here: they are critical of the notion that love is something that simply happens to us (or does not), in which we have and can have no guiding hand.[78]

Happily, I think that we can preserve the notion that working at love is both necessary and praiseworthy, without abandoning the sorts of insights into love's essential self-forgetfulness that we find in the writings of Hauskeller and

Ferraro. The only concession we will need to make is that, while some *ways* of working at love are appropriate, others are not. What counts as appropriate will, understandably, in part be determined by the sort of thing that love is. And we will see that, at least on the face of it, there is a case for saying that the use of love drugs to reignite or maintain love falls into the 'inappropriate' camp.

So, at what precisely must one work, when working at love? A hint can be gained from a paper by Lotte Spreeuwenberg and Katrien Schaubroeck. Spreeuwenberg and Schaubroeck understand love as a practice, rather than primarily as a mental state. In fleshing out just what sort of practice it is, they draw heavily on the work of Iris Murdoch, whose account of love fits well with much of what I have just said: 'For Murdoch, loving consists in looking outside oneself, focussing our attention to [*sic*] the particular and the unique.'[79] It is, then, 'a practice of self-transcendence',[80] of fully comprehending, valuing, and opening up to the individual and independent reality of another. This is what leads Murdoch to make her famous pronouncement that 'Love is the extremely difficult realisation that something other than oneself is real.'[81] Like all difficult things, it requires effort, but effort of a particular sort, and in a particular direction. If my relationship with my partner is failing, what I really need to do, on this understanding, is not primarily to focus on moulding some psychological state of mine, but rather to *see her* more clearly. Of course, if I succeed in doing this, the quality of my attention will have changed, and there will therefore be an alteration in an aspect of my inner life. But the change will come about not as a result of turning away from the world into the inner realm and directly manipulating my own psychology; it will instead accompany my attending fully, and opening up, to something entirely outside myself. In other words, although the work will be carried out *in* my psyche, it will not self-consciously be work *on* my psyche. Even though I may end up in a desirable state, the goal of my effort is not to end up in a desirable state. This self-transcending practice of focussing my attention wholly on another – an act of 'unselfing' as Murdoch would have it – is love, according to Spreeuwenberg and Schaubroeck.

The parallel with what Wolf has to say about love and its importance should be clear. The lover in the Murdochian picture is 'rooted, motivationally, to the world', to something (someone) entirely independent of her and her own patterns of self-interest. But there is a further similarity in the work of both thinkers. To the extent that we love successfully, thinks Murdoch, we can be said to be free. What we are free *of* in such a situation is the demands of the 'fat relentless ego'[82] and the falsifying veil that it places between us and the world, whereby the world comes to be grasped not as it is in itself, but merely as something that can serve or frustrate our own interests. Love pierces that veil, and connects us to the independent being and inherent value of another person, not merely her value *to us*. Wolf's account of freedom is not dissimilar to this. Freedom, according to her, is not a matter of self-creation or self-determination, nor even especially of control; rather, it is a matter of one's action being guided by a clear apprehension of reality. To be rooted motivationally to the world *as it is* (a state that Wolf calls, employing a rather specialized sense of the expression, 'sanity'), is to be free.[83]

It is potentially enlightening to contrast this Murdochian/Wolfian conception of freedom with the sort of freedom that our authors think technologies such as love drugs can deliver. Their favoured conception is not one of freedom from self-interest, but freedom from the dominion of our evolved nature, allowing for the unhampered satisfaction of our preferences. Such freedom involves our gaining control over our biological natures and making them work to serve our own ends. In Section 6.2, I will point out some unfortunate consequences of the drive for freedom understood in this way. For now, we need only note the contrast with the Murdochian/Wolfian account.

We may balk at the suggestion that striving to achieve a clear vision of a partner is the sole work that we might put into maintaining or strengthening a relationship, even if it is a substantial or even the central part of the picture. At any rate, our authors mention several other means of strengthening romantic attachment, none of which seems ethically questionable. Oxytocin is released – and thus either attachment strengthened, other things being equal, or some condition that constitutes fertile ground for attachment produced – when we engage in intimate touch (massage, for example), have sex, hold hands, and so on. If a couple were to try further to embed their relationship by having sex (or even holding hands!) more often, we would not think there was anything wrong with that.

Nothing wrong, perhaps. But we might wonder whether there is something a little peculiar or misconceived about it: some element of putting the cart before the horse. As McGee points out, within a relationship, we are not apt to think of lovemaking (or hand-holding) as a means of increasing attachment, nor to engage in it with that aim in mind; rather, we see it as an *expression* of romantic attachment or love. Its role 'is not wholly causal but is rather a consequence of the love shared between the partners'.[84] Note that McGee says its role is not *wholly* causal. He does not deny, then, that lovemaking has (or at any rate can have – there are romantic relationships in which sex plays no part) a role in deepening attachment and thereby strengthening a relationship. Nor does he deny that it has that role because it triggers the action of oxytocin. His suggestion, I think – and it is certainly mine – is that in the normal run of things we do not consciously employ sex within a relationship with that goal in mind, and to do so would seem in some measure to demote the activity from its accustomed role as an expression of love. Compare the role of gratitude in friendship: regular expressions of gratitude will typically serve to strengthen a friendship, but we do not tend to express gratitude *in order* to deepen our friendships. There might be something odd – something a little too calculating or mercenary – in our doing so.

If there is something strange about the idea of making love specifically in order to boost attachment, it seems to me that the peculiarity only deepens if we start to think of and engage in the activity under the description 'a means of boosting oxytocin'. And yet, this is how, according to Earp and Savulescu's book, an anonymous woman describes matters in an online comment on one of our authors' pieces:

> I just rounded the corner of my 4th year of marriage, and my husband is in his 3rd year of a medical residency – I see him awake 3x a week if I'm lucky. And that awake time usually translates to dinner, conversation, and then sleep. You know what that means? Unless I'm immediately stripping off both our clothes to have sex I'm not really in the mood for (or he isn't really in the mood for; his job is very stressful!), *we may get a single release of oxytocin (from sex/touching) a week*. That makes you feel really unconnected to a partner, even if you talk . . . and touch as often as you can [emphasis added].[85]

I should strongly emphasize that, in suggesting there is a slightly off-kilter tone to the italicized part of this quotation, I am not at all concerned to criticize its author. The quotation as a whole tells us, I think, something very regrettable about contemporary life and, in particular, the culture of the modern workplace. There can be little doubt that conditions such as the ones the author describes make the maintenance of close relationships challenging. And, even though I find it odd to conceptualize sex as a means of boosting oxytocin, I do not blame her for thinking of it in that way, partially given her situation, but mainly given the intellectual context created by work on the neurology of love and discussions about the possibility of love drugs.

That is, we are encouraged to think of an area of our life that matters hugely to us in terms that belong properly to the scientific image of humankind-in-the-world. That is not altogether inappropriate, and certainly is not remotely inaccurate: throughout our discussion, we have been taking it as a given that neurochemistry is heavily implicated in the phenomena of love and attachment. And yet taking some description that belongs to the scientific rather than the manifest image as a goal of a very *personal* activity creates a jarring effect. Conceptualizing the ends of lovemaking in terms of neurochemistry introduces into an activity that gains its whole meaning for us from the sorts of person-based concepts that hold sway in the manifest image, sub-personal, scientific-image ways of understanding ourselves, which pull in a different direction. Some possible dangers of this sort of cross-image reductionism will be detailed in Section 6.2.

Let us take a step back. The claim that I have made – guided by thinkers such as Hauskeller, Ferraro, Spreeuwenberg and Schaubroeck, Murdoch, and Wolf – is that although work and effort are definitely needed in the sphere of love, that work should not have as its goal the production of a desirable state in oneself; such work pulls in the opposite direction from that involved in maintaining love. There was no suggestion in the case of John that he took his being in the state of loving Jim to have anything other than intrinsic value. And yet still, it seems, his object in considering the use of love drugs was at odds with the object of love: he was taking the state of loving to be what is primarily of intrinsic value, whereas the lover accords that primary value to the beloved. However, the sort of problem I have been pointing towards is perhaps most vividly apparent in cases where, unlike John, one wishes to be in a loving relationship in order to gain the various hedonic and health benefits that accompany love. In that sort of situation, one is according love an instrumental value. Loving is a state that it is good to be in, chiefly because it leads to one's possession of other goods that are intrinsically valuable.

As noted earlier, our authors often display a tendency to place the instrumental value of love very much in the foreground, sometimes to the detriment of any intrinsic value that it might be thought to have. Indeed, as Sven Nyholm has noted,[86] even when they mention its intrinsic value, they are apt, inconsistently, to slide into giving an instrumental justification of it. Here is the passage from the authors' work that Nyholm has in mind:

> Relationships may also [in addition to being regarded as instrumentally valuable, insofar as they have health and hedonic benefits] be viewed as good in themselves, either as something valuable in addition to the joy they bring the partners, or as something that even transcends their well-being (e.g. as a means of self-development, self-realisation or even duty to a divine plan).[87]

It is noteworthy how swiftly this supposed account of love's intrinsic value collapses into a list of ends to which love is a means.

Now, if John were to accord merely instrumental value to his loving Jim (or even a hidden kind of instrumental value that masquerades as intrinsic value, as in the passage just quoted), then it would seem that there undoubtedly is a clash between the focus of genuine love, on the one hand, and the sort of self-interested goal he is chasing in attempting to rekindle love on the other. It would be as if someone were to seek friendship with a rich person, simply in the hope that they may receive a handout; it is clear that what they sought would not really be friendship. However, it is possible to imagine the proponent of love drugs agreeing with this and yet being unconcerned. The clash, she may say, will be short-lived, provided that conditions line up in such a way that the drugs do their job.

To explain: John admittedly has a self-interested aim in taking love drugs. He no longer loves Jim, but he values the state of loving Jim that he used to enjoy. He wants to regain that state, either because the state leads to benefits (happiness, contentment, good health, and so on), or because, all by itself, it constitutes a benefit. Now, let us suppose that he takes the drugs and that by whatever means – whether directly or indirectly – they succeed in propelling him back into his desired state. If that *genuinely* happens, then John will find that his focus is no longer on being in the state, but is instead firmly back on Jim, precisely because he is now *in* the state. That is, the action of the drugs will have shifted him from a situation in which what he primarily values is the lost state of loving Jim, into a situation where he once again primarily values Jim. He will then have gained the state he desired, and it is a state in which being in the state itself seems much less important to him than Jim does.

Is this a convincing response to the worries expressed by the likes of Hauskeller and Ferraro? I do not think that it is, even though it may initially appear persuasive. Let us recall what administering oxytocin is supposed to do, other things being equal. At the most, it produces or strengthens attachment; at the least, it produces some facilitative state (which we earlier dubbed 'factor F') that allows attachment to develop. Those who, unlike Fisher, see a distinction between attachment and love (such as our authors), will maintain that it cannot directly produce love. And attachment does not necessarily have the self-forgetting quality of love: one may be attached to another for all sorts of self-serving reasons. When it lacks self-forgetfulness, and you have produced it because it is a state that you wanted to be in rather than because you were wholly focussed on its object, it may get in the way of, and thereby preclude, the sort of valuing of its object that is distinctive of romantic love.

To be clear: attachment of course involves a focus on its object. If it did not, it would not be attachment – one cannot sensibly aim at being in a state of attachment without aiming to be in a state that focuses on an object. So, my point is not that, in aiming at that state, one will somehow end up in it while feeling no particular way about its object. That would be an impossibility. But what one might end up primarily valuing is one's gaining certain benefits – emotional, financial, hedonic, prestige-related, and so on – from standing in a particular relationship to that object. There is such a thing as being attached selfishly. Arguably, there is no such thing as loving selfishly; though people sometimes talk as if there is, there is a suspicion that they are misapplying the criteria for something's counting as love. An unshakeable aura of oxymoron seems to me, at any rate, to attach to the expression 'selfish love'.

Of course, the idea behind embedding attachment through the use of love drugs is presumably that, since attachment underpins love, its presence will supply fertile soil in which love can then develop or re-emerge. But I think we can be sceptical whether a self-concerned attachment – an attachment sought largely because the agent wants for whatever reason to be in a state of attachment or, indeed, a state of love – will constitute the right sort of soil for the growth of a wholly other-directed state.

Nonetheless, it is possible to envision a fairly restricted but still significant range of cases that would not be problematic in the ways sketched above. Let us imagine a third couple, Jamal and Joanna. Their relationship is under siege: both are aware that Jamal's attachment is diminishing. He still loves Joanna, but that love is in a parlous condition. They are only too aware that if they do not take action soon, it may not be long before it disappears altogether. Both are alarmed at this prospect, and alarmed at it precisely because, at the moment, they still love each other. Jamal values his love for Joanna and does so not simply because it is a state that he would like himself to be in, but because, first and foremost, he values Joanna herself in ways that are distinctive of romantic love. It is just that he does not value her in this way quite as much as he used to. Perhaps there are days when he seems not to at all, and they are getting more frequent. They are both sensible that the clock is ticking on the relationship.

Jamal is also aware that the person he values intrinsically, *qua* beloved, values the love that he has for her. Because of the way in which he values Joanna, he wants her to continue to experience that love indefinitely and not have it fizzle out in the next few months or years. As they have tried everything else that is available to them, Jamal suggests that he try love drugs: an oxytocin nasal spray, perhaps, in combination with the sort of relationship therapy that has previously, when pursued on its own, proved ineffective. He wants to strengthen his attachment to Joanna, but the reason he wants to do this, again, is because he loves her. Here, his aim does not seem to be a self-interested one at all, and so it seems perfectly possible that, for him and for Joanna, creating a more solid bed of attachment will enable the further development of his love.

The upshot is that although in many cases the use of love drugs might be at odds with the focus of love, this need not be the case in all relationships. What starts in self-interest is likely to end in self-interest; what starts in love (as Jamal's taking love drugs will) need not. But even then, some further, vitally important questions remain. Suppose that something that looks very like strengthened love for Joanna results from Jamal's taking love drugs. Is that 'love' authentic?

Is Joanna justified in valuing the fact that she is the object of it? And though, as a more or less direct result of taking the drugs, Jamal now values Joanna in ways distinctive of romantic love in a more settled manner, can we be sure that he has *reason* to value her in this way, and reason to value his valuing her?

6 In Search of True Love: The Issue of Authenticity

Perhaps unsurprisingly, a lot of the critical literature that has grown up around our authors' work has focussed on the question of whether a love born of, or sustained by, love drugs will be the real deal. Will the 'love' that results from the use of drugs be authentic? Faced with this question, the authors have made, broadly, two responses. First, they have argued that there is no reason to suppose that chemically boosted love will be in any way inauthentic. Secondly, they have asked whether, even if it were, that would really matter. I will be dealing with the former response at some length throughout the current section. First, however, I want to address their suggestion that it may not matter, or more accurately may not matter *overall*, if we produce inauthentic love. This suggestion, I think, rests on a confusion.

In tackling the issue of authenticity, the authors seem not to have a settled idea of what precisely their critics think might be rendered inauthentic by the use of love drugs. In their initial paper in 2008, Savulescu and Sandberg pose the question in this way: 'Would chemical enhancement of relations render love inauthentic?' However, in a 2015 paper on the medicalization of love, Earp, Sandberg, and Savulescu take the question to be whether the love-enhanced *self* would be inauthentic – here, they leave the question of *love*'s authenticity aside. Both papers, nonetheless, share a response to the issue: both ask whether authenticity should be thought of as invariably trumping other values. So, in the 2008 paper, the authors write, 'Even if love were not authentic, authenticity is not an overriding or exclusive value. People can trade a degree of authenticity for other values in their lives.'[88] In 2015, they say:

> [I]t is unclear whether, even if [the administration of love drugs] did pose such a threat, this would entail that it should not be done (under the right kinds of conditions). Indeed, one might wish to consider a more basic issue, which is to ask exactly what the value of authenticity is – and how it weighs against other values. Perhaps it is authentic for a person to be sad and sullen, withdrawn and incommunicative, or cold, unapproachable, and unloving. Yet within the hierarchy of values for a particular couple, a happy or well-functioning relationship may be more important than an abstract notion of authenticity.[89]

It is possible that the notions of love's authenticity and the authenticity of the lover are in some way intertwined; indeed, some of what I have to say in the following sub-sections, and particularly in Section 6.2, will at least imply that this is the case. For now, though, for the sake of simplicity, I would like to focus primarily on the issue of the authenticity specifically of love.

The authors seem to think that one's concern with the authenticity of love might be rooted in one's valuing and being committed to authenticity in the abstract. This then enables them to question whether authenticity is an *overriding* value: whether, for example, a happy and well-functioning relationship might, in some people's eyes at least, be of greater value. Why assume that authenticity is necessarily at the top of a hierarchy of values?

This response, I think, embodies a significant mistake. If, following Jamal's use of love drugs, Joanna is concerned with the question of whether his rejuvenated love for her is authentic, her concern derives from the fact that she values love, rather than that she values authenticity in the abstract. In general, if you genuinely value x, you will be concerned that any putative instance of x you encounter or possess is authentic, simply because you value x, and not primarily because you value authenticity. A carpenter wants to be sure that the hammer in her toolbox is an authentic hammer, rather than, say, a rubber hammer placed there by her mischievous child. Her concern derives from the fact that she has a professional investment in having functioning tools to hand, not from an overwhelming commitment to authenticity in the abstract.[90] If the latter were her main interest, would she not be as content to find an authentic grilled cheese sandwich in her toolbox as an authentic hammer?

Now, if a couple is attempting to revivify or strengthen love through the use of drugs, we can take it that they value the prospect of their love's being revivified or strengthened. In the very act of authentically valuing love, what they are valuing, and therefore aiming at, is authentic love. They are not valuing and striving for two things: love and, perhaps as an optional extra, authenticity. It would make no sense for them to say 'All we want here is a loving relationship – it is a matter of indifference to us whether it is an authentic one, because frankly authenticity does not occupy a particularly elevated place in our hierarchy of values.' If this were earnestly uttered, it would only serve to show that the couple was not overly concerned to have a loving relationship after all. It would be like saying 'It is a very hot day, and all I want is an ice-cream cone – I am unconcerned with whether it is real, or a plastic representation of an ice-cream cone.'

If one is authentically aiming at x, that it should be an authentic x is not an optional extra. If one is authentically aiming at love, that the outcome should be authentic love is, likewise, not something with which one can be unconcerned. With that much agreed, there is of course still a question to be asked about whether a love fostered or stabilized through the use of love drugs would or would not be authentic. It is to this crucial issue that I now turn.

That the use of love drugs would not lead to authentic love, or at least not to the particular intrinsic good that we typically seek in love, is the central claim of Sven Nyholm's 2015 paper, 'Love troubles: Human attachment and biomedical enhancements'. As mentioned in Section 5, in setting out what he takes to be the *way* in which we value love, and *what it is* about love that we value, Nyholm concentrates almost exclusively on the perspective of the beloved *qua* beloved.[91] He does not explicitly state his rationale for this approach, though his emphasis harmonizes with my claim that the lover *qua* lover does not primarily value her own love, but rather her beloved. Thus, perhaps if we want to say something significant about the value of romantic love, it makes sense to focus on the perspective from which love is what is primarily valued: namely, the standpoint of the beloved *qua* beloved. Even so, part of Nyholm's account of what matters to the beloved is that her lover should endorse, and therefore value, the love he or she feels for her (which is why I say that his focus on what the beloved values is *almost* exclusive). This dovetails neatly with my view that, as a secondary phenomenon, the lover will ideally value her own valuing of the beloved in ways distinctive of romantic love.

Nyholm maintains that, at least in contemporary Western culture, the value that romantic love holds for the beloved is intrinsic rather than instrumental. He suggests that the reason our authors feel able to endorse the use of love drugs is in part because they place undue emphasis on the extrinsic benefits that accrue from loving or being loved. But to accord merely instrumental value to love – or at least to foreground such value – is, as Nyholm tells us in another paper, to be guilty of an 'evaluative category mistake'.[92] It is to miss what it is about love (that is, *being* loved) that we value in valuing it.

So, what is it that we value in being the object of a romantic partner's love, if not the hedonic and health benefits that accompany it? Why can what we value not be provided by our lover's making use of love drugs? In order to answer the former question, Nyholm appeals to Philip Pettit's account of love as a robust good:[93]

> [T]o enjoy somebody's love, it must be, Pettit claims, that we can count on their care across various different situations and scenarios, and not just in the actual circumstances we find ourselves in [this, in Pettit's terms, is what makes love a robustly demanding good]. 'Love is not love', Pettit quotes Shakespeare as musing, 'which alters, when it alteration finds'. The attachment of another must, in other words, be firm and robust in order for us to enjoy the good of their love. If they were to withdraw their care and concern as soon as providing it might be slightly inopportune for them, we would not enjoy their love, but rather some other, 'thinner' good.[94]

Now, as Nyholm is quick to point out, if all there were to love was its robustly demanding nature, then we might think that love drugs could be regarded as an unequivocally good thing. After all, their function will be to make attachment much more robust: firmer, less likely to fade, more within the control of the lover, and so on.

Nonetheless, Nyholm points out, there are two further properties, beyond its robustness, that an attachment must have if it is to possess the features the beloved values in the love she receives. It must proceed from some factor internal to the lover, and that factor must have a particularistic focus. More precisely, as Nyholm writes:

> There is ... supposed to be some inner state, disposition, or attitude on the part of the lover that generates the robustly available care and affection. And it is supposed to be that it is us in particular that our lover homes in on, such that it is we as the particular people that we are who are able to call forth, activate, or inspire this internal disposition of the lover.[95]

So, what the beloved values in her lover's love is at least in part (but necessarily) that she, the beloved, is able to inspire it all by herself. It is she alone, as the particular person she is, who triggers in her lover the disposition to offer care, concern, affection, and so on. In keeping with what we have said so far, we might perhaps characterize things in this way: it is she alone who is able to evoke in the lover a disposition to value her intrinsically, in ways distinctive of romantic love. For ease of reference, we can call this the particularity requirement, and set it out as follows:

> **The particularity requirement:** If A loves B, then A's attachment is triggered by B's being the particular person that B is.

At first sight, it perhaps seems clear why the use of love drugs to sustain attachment would fall foul of the particularity requirement. When such drugs are used, we might want to say, it is the drug that is ultimately responsible for A's attachment to B (in the sense that, whether the productive or the facilitative account is correct, the attachment would not exist had the drug not been used), rather than B's being the particular person she is. However, that might not be the most accurate way of describing the situation. When A has used love drugs, A's attachment is still to B in particular: the drugs do not render A hopelessly attached also to C, D, E, and so on. All the drugs have done, we might want to say, is put A into a state in which B is able, being the particular person that B is, to trigger A's attachment (through, for example, producing in A a 'pro-relationship mindset' or a tendency to see certain social cues as salient[96]).

Pettit would counter by saying that the pharmaceutically provoked attachment lacks the requisite robustness to count as love: it will not be present in altered circumstances in which the drugs have not been used. In a passage quoted by Nyholm, Pettit writes:

Puck, Shakespeare's elf in *A Midsummer Night's Dream*, does not induce love in his victims as he mesmerizes random couples into doting on one another. Would your love be available to me if your care depended on the hypnotic influence of Puck's spell? No, because that spell would not make your care robust over scenarios where there is no constraint, and so no spell, at the origin of your care. It would not constitute love but only an imperfect simulacrum.[97]

Even leaving aside Pettit's shaky memory of which class of supernatural being Puck belongs to, it seems possible not to be much impressed by this response, at least in so far as we can apply it – as Nyholm presumably wants to – to the sphere of love drugs rather than of spells and magic potions. The case we are imagining is one in which, say, the lover's disposition is anchored in the presence of exogenous oxytocin. It is true that were that exogenous oxytocin not present, the disposition would not be in place either. So, the care that the lover offers is not robust over scenarios in which exogenous oxytocin is not present. But then, in the normal run of things – where romantic attachment arises naturally – we are taking it that such attachment is anchored in endogenous oxytocin. And in such cases, which we can sensibly regard as paradigmatic, undisputed instances of romantic love, the attachment is not robust across scenarios where endogenous oxytocin (and, for that matter, exogenous oxytocin) is absent. And yet we do not want to say this: 'There is no love in place here, just because the attachment does not exist at close possible worlds in which oxytocin is not doing its work.' To do so would be to commit ourselves to the absurd view that nobody has ever loved anybody.

What is more, Nyholm's own position cannot, or at least for the sake of consistency *should* not, mirror Pettit's in this respect. Recall that Nyholm thinks effective love drugs, far from stripping attachment of robustness, will in fact promise to make it more robust than it would otherwise be. So, a lack of robustness is not what makes it the case that authentic love is absent when love drugs are used; what is more, as we have seen, the particularity requirement is not violated by their use. And yet, as Nyholm maintains, many people have a strong intuition that whatever is produced by the use of love drugs is not the real thing, but at best a counterfeit. Of course, not everybody has such an intuition. Although I can report, in the interests of full disclosure, that I do; in the course of teaching on this topic I have spoken to numerous students who do not. If the intuition is to carry any weight, it needs not simply to be shown to exist in some people, nor even to be widespread, but to be backed up with a rational justification. I think it probable that this can be done, but we will need to work slowly towards it. With that aim in mind, I want first to propose, and subsequently to argue for, a slight but significant revision of the particularity requirement. Let us call the revised principle the dual-particularity requirement:

The dual-particularity requirement: If A loves B, then A's attachment is triggered by (1) B's being the particular person that B is, in virtue of (2) A's being the particular person that A is.

The thought here is that a full account of an instance of romantic love between A and B cannot stop at an explanation of the features of B that call forth the loving response in A; it must also reference what it is about A as the particular person A is that makes A respond in that way. Montaigne explains why he loved a departed friend with the words, 'Because it was him: because it was me.'[98] Perhaps Montaigne thinks that this can be the *whole* explanation. Happily, the dual-particularity requirement does not commit us to that view; nor, I think, should we adopt it. And yet there is something right about what he says. His friend's having been the particular person he was called forth a certain response in Montaigne, but a proper account of that response needs also to make mention of what *in Montaigne* enabled it.

We might think that Nyholm demonstrates in his paper that he is committed to the dual-particularity requirement. That is, following Pettit he mentions the internal factor that a lover A must possess, such that that factor is focussed on and called into being by the beloved B as the particular person B is. And that internal factor, we might think, is what is referred to under clause (2) of the dual-particularity requirement. However, Nyholm identifies A's internal factor with a disposition to offer robust care and affection to B, where that disposition is called forth by B's being the particular person that B is. Let us give this disposition, which is triggered by B, a label: let us call it D_1. What we need to understand clause (2) of the dual-particularity requirement to be referencing is not D_1, but what it is about A that makes it the case that B is capable of triggering D_1's existence. What is it, in other words, about A that makes A respond to B in the way that A does? What is it about A that bestows on B the power to generate D_1 in A? That factor in A cannot be D_1. After all, D_1 cannot generate *itself*. It seems, then, that it must be a second-order disposition to respond to B by becoming disposed (through the formation of D_1) to offer robust care and affection to B. Let us call this second-order disposition D_2.

In the normal run of things, absent the use of love drugs, A's possession of D_2 will be dependent on certain constitutional facts about A (temperament, personality, values, preferences, and so on). These constitutional facts will make it the case that certain sets of features that belong to B are reasons for A's being lovingly attached to B and have come to be seen as such reasons by A. The appeal to particular constitutional facts about A here is designed to capture the truth that what might function as reasons for A to be lovingly attached to B might not function as, say, reasons for C, D, or E to be lovingly attached to

B. Therein lies one of the particularities referenced in the dual-particularity requirement.

Assuming that love drugs – exogenous oxytocin, for example – can indeed help reignite or strengthen attachment (at the very least by means of producing some other, facilitative state), what they must do in order to work is play some sort of role in bringing about D_1. So, let us suppose that Jamal's use of love drugs to put his loving attachment to Joanna back on track succeeds. What the drugs do in that case is in some way help to stabilize, strengthen, or reinforce Jamal's D_1 with regard to Joanna. When we consider what has happened to Jamal in this case, there seem to be three possibilities:

(1) D_1 has been directly produced by the love drugs, in the absence of D_2 being operative in Jamal (in other words, Jamal lacks *in himself* the disposition to form, or perhaps maintain, a disposition to offer robust care and affection to Joanna; nonetheless, a disposition to offer robust care and affection is pharmaceutically induced). This possibility is consistent with the productive account of the action of endomimetic love drugs and may be in place if that account is correct.

(2) The love drugs produce or strengthen D_2 in Jamal, by (re-)instigating features of Joanna as reasons that motivate the generation of D_1. (So, qualities of Joanna that had once been reasons for Jamal's loving attachment have ceased to be so, at least in any substantial way; the action of the love drugs reinstates them as full-blooded reasons – either *ab initio* or by altering Jamal's constitution in some way – that then anchor the disposition to supply robust care and affection.) This possibility is consistent with, and indeed strongly suggests, certain versions of the facilitative account of the action of endomimetic love drugs: namely, the version of the facilitative account that sees such drugs as productive of a 'pro-relationship mindset' or the version that makes certain stimuli appear salient to the subject. It may also be consistent with the productive account, if we see that account as allowing apparent reasons for attachment to be produced *alongside* attachment.

(3) The love drugs produce or strengthen D_2 in Jamal by allowing him to see that features of Joanna remain (that is, always have been, given certain facts about his constitution) reasons for him to have attitudes of robust care and affection towards her, even though he had ceased to regard them in that way. In other words, the drugs work by opening his eyes to the fact that Joanna's qualities have never ceased to be reasons for him to be lovingly attached to her; he has come erroneously not to see things that way, perhaps because his Murdochian attention to Joanna has atrophied somewhat over the years. This possibility is consistent with the facilitative account in all its

forms. Clearly, it is consistent with that version of the account that understands oxytocin as productive of nothing more than improved communication. But it is also consistent, as we saw in Sections 4.2 and 4.3, with the other two versions of the facilitative account, provided that the facilitating factor F in both cases does nothing more than help reveal reasons that the subject genuinely has, but of which they have for some reason or other been ignorant.

6.1 Assuming That Possibility (1) Obtains

Suppose first that (1) is the case. In a scenario where love drugs produced D_1 in Jamal without D_2 being in place, his attachment to Joanna would not be based on reasons. It seems plausible to maintain that in that case, the attachment would fall short of love. It might be more worthy of being called infatuation. We typically take it, I think, that if A loves B, A should be able to give an account of the reasons *why* A loves B, or at the very least that such reasons should be in place even if they are somehow inarticulable.

Be that as it may, it seems that attachment that does not qualify as love is certainly a possibility, even without the use of love drugs, and indeed we have seen that our authors believe this to be the case too, given their opposition to phase reductionism. The suggestion I am making here is that, whether or not love is simply equivalent to reason-directed attachment, or whether there is something more to love than that, still an attachment that is not based on or directed by reasons cannot count as love. Certainly, it seems that Joanna, as the object of such attachment, will not, to borrow Nyholm's phrase, enjoy the intrinsic good of love. If she were to know that Jamal was attached to her without having any reason to be so attached, she would likely not find much to value in that state of affairs, especially if what she was hoping for was to be the object of his love on account of her being the particular person she is. And when it comes to Jamal's perspective on the situation, although he will *ex hypothesi* be attached to Joanna, it is doubtful whether he should endorse or value an attachment that is not adequately backed by reasons. It may be objected that it is built into the example that Jamal does have at least some vestigial reasons for his attachment: he still loves Joanna, even though he is aware that that love is inexorably fading. But the point is that, if (1) is the case, there is a strengthening of attachment with no corresponding strengthening of reasons. All the additional attachment brought about by the love drugs is, so to speak, outside the reach of reasons. What reasons there are, are not brought about or strengthened by the action of the drugs. It would be easy, then, to see that action as bringing about no real improvement.

6.2 Assuming That Possibility (2) Obtains

If what is wanted in possibility (1) is reasons, perhaps possibility (2) will fare better. If that possibility is actual, Jamal's taking love drugs will reinvigorate his waning attachment to Joanna by supplying him with new or strengthened reasons for that attachment. That is, he will now find certain things about Joanna romantically salient, so to speak, which he either did not find thus salient before or had ceased to find fully salient. A pharmaceutically modified D_2 will, in this scenario, take root in Jamal, allowing certain facts about Joanna as the particular person she is to trigger and ground D_1.

On the face of it, then, (2) appears a much more promising possibility than (1). And it might also seem to have potential when we dig a little deeper, by considering the outline of an argument from Robbie Arrell against the use of a certain sort of love drug.[99] Arrell asks us to imagine a situation in which a husband, Harry, has been unfaithful to his wife Karen and, in the hope of maintaining sexual fidelity in the future, takes a drug, Lupron, that will considerably decrease or extinguish his desire for sex with women other than his wife. Insofar as that drug will decrease his desire for others, our authors might classify it as an anti-love drug, and insofar as it promotes sexual fidelity, they might want to call it a love drug proper. (We need not, for our purposes here, be distracted by the likelihood that Lupron will also decrease or extinguish Harry's desire for sex with Karen.)

Arrell's argument against Harry's using Lupron is detailed and subtle, but the upshot of it is that Karen is unlikely to feel her vulnerability to harm from Harry has been suitably attenuated by his taking Lupron. The outcome of his previous infidelity, Arrell tells us, is this:

> Karen's confidence that Harry is appropriately disposed to be robustly faithful to her (of which she previously felt reasonably assured) is shattered. Importantly, what Karen loses confidence in is not Harry's disposition to be faithful *as such*. Rather, what she is stripped of is the confidence she had (pre-affair) that Harry's disposition to be faithful is sufficient to ensure he robustly refrains from engaging in extra-marital sex .... To give their marriage a fighting chance, then, it is imperative the couple alight on a therapy regime that not only promotes the probability that, in future, Harry will be faithful, but also (and crucially) restores Karen's confidence that he is appropriately disposed to be.[100]

The reason the situation is not helped by Harry's taking Lupron, then, is that it is a mechanical, non-cognitive intervention: a pharmaceutical straitjacket that bears comparison to Odysseus' being bound to his ship's mast in order not to be lured by the sirens' song. It does not change his underlying disposition. At least, we might want to say, using our own terminology, that it alters his D_1 in certain ways, without altering his D_2. *He* as a person, so to speak, comes out of the intervention unchanged. What was needed in order to attenuate Karen's vulnerability was not this sort of intervention, but a cognitive fix of the sort promised by relationship therapy: something that could touch and change the sorts of things he counts as reasons to act, and thus alter *him*, rather than simply constraining his behaviour (albeit along desirable dimensions).

We might want to object at this point that our authors would be unlikely to sanction the use of Lupron alone to address Harry's issues with fidelity. They would want, that is, to see it used in combination with just the sort of relationship therapy Arrell favours, increasing the chances of that cognitive intervention's succeeding. However, Arrell thinks that such a combined approach will do nothing to attenuate Karen's vulnerability, since even if it is successful the epistemic waters will have been irremediably muddied by the use of Lupron. That is, Karen will not know whether Harry's improved behaviour is a result of the cognitive element of the treatment – and so represents a change in him – or of the mechanical element.

Now, if we extrapolate from Arrell's particular argument, and apply his findings to Jamal and Joanna's case, it might seem that they render possibility (2) unobjectionable. Jamal has not been unfaithful to Joanna and is taking oxytocin rather than Lupron. If possibility (2) is actual, Jamal himself has been changed by the successful intervention, as Harry was not in taking Lupron. Jamal's D_2 has been altered, in such a way that he has reasons for attachment to Joanna that he did not have before, and those reasons now anchor his D_1. And this change is not merely mechanical, but cognitive – Jamal sees the world, or that part of the world that is Joanna, differently. Features of Joanna, as the particular person she is, are now salient for him, in a way they were not before. What is more, if the oxytocin is administered in combination with relationship therapy, Joanna is not subject to any epistemic uncertainty of the sort faced by Karen, just because both treatment modalities work by affecting the cognitive. So, all is well, surely, if (2) is the case?

I want to suggest that perhaps all is not well. The misgivings I want to express are quite difficult to articulate, but they revolve around the fact that, if possibility (2) is in place, while the effects of the drug are cognitive, its action in producing those cognitive effects is mechanical. That is, it functions not by leading people to see certain considerations as reasons for them to be attached, in the way that relationship therapy might, but by strong-arming them into seeing those considerations as salient. Although the facilitative account is distinct from the productive, we need to be aware that it still portrays oxytocin as productive of *something*: namely, the facilitative factor *F*, whatever that may be. Where F is a propensity for coming to have new reasons, as some of the scientific literature suggests it is – through the alteration of a subject's 'mind-set', or through making certain stimuli salient for them – there is arguably cause for concern. Under possibility (2), use of love drugs like oxytocin seems to represent, to resort to Sellarsian language again, a questionable incursion of the realm of law (the mechanical realm, if you like) into the space of reasons. We might worry that the reasons Jamal has following the use of the drug are not in any full-blooded sense really *his* reasons. They have not been arrived at due to particular native constitutional facts about him, as happens in the case of an unenhanced D_2, nor has he been led to them by following the implications of reasons that are uncontroversially his own, as may happen in relationship therapy. Rather, they have, in a manner of speaking, simply been foisted upon him. Consider Titania on being subjected to Puck's love potion; she perhaps now sees reasons to find a weaver with a donkey's head adorable, but they are not the reasons of a Queen of the Fairies. There is no deductive or inductive route from the reasons that anchor her love for Oberon to reasons to be attracted to a braying rustic with furry ears.

If this is what happens, it is hard to see how Joanna is in a much better situation under possibility (2) than she would be under possibility (1). That is, it seems that having someone attached to you for reasons that are not his own, that have merely been induced in him, does not have many advantages over his being attached to you for no reason at all. It is perhaps equally difficult to see why Jamal would endorse his own attachment to Joanna. Why would he value his own valuing of Joanna, when the reasons for which he values her are not his own but have been chemically foisted upon him? And certainly, it seems that under possibility (2), the spirit if not the letter of the dual-particularity requirement's second clause is violated. In a sense, of course, it *is* because of something about Jamal's being the particular person he is that he is attached to Joanna. He is someone who has taken love drugs and mechanically made it the case that certain features of Joanna have a salience for him that they previously lacked. But in another sense, since the reasons he has are reasons that are not really his own – reasons into which he has been chemically strong-armed – it is not really something authentically about him that makes him regard Joanna in the way he now does.

If that last argument is not seen as sufficiently compelling (though I suspect it should be), there is I think a deeper point to be made about the violation of the dual-particularity requirement under possibility (2). We are imagining a situation in which, through the deliberate use of the chemicals implicated in romantic attachment, we manipulate the sorts of considerations that count as reasons for us to be attached. We can, in a manner of speaking and at least to some extent, be in control of *who we are* as a partner or (if you like) a romantic agent. The question then arises: who is the self that chooses what should strike us as reasons for attachment? Who are we when we are deciding who to be? The act of choice here seems necessarily to involve an abstraction from the particular self we as a matter of fact are, in order to decide which particular self to be. We conceive of ourselves as retreating, then, into a featureless, unembedded, perhaps *noumenal* self that is devoid of all particularity, a pure locus of choice. This is a perspective that, arguably, is involved in any thought of enhancing what we are (in terms of character, reasons, values, and so on, even if not somatically), but it is one that is uniquely damaging to any supposed enhancements to our capacity to love another individual. The project of enhancing love, if possibility (2) is actual, ultimately de-particularizes the person seeking the enhancement, forcing a self-conception that undercuts the possibility of love by violating the second clause of the dual-particularity requirement.

Part of the problem here might be that the use of love drugs, if possibility (2) holds, compels us to adopt a pernicious cross-image reductionism of the sort set out in Section 3.5. That is, we want to take control of an aspect of ourselves that shows up only at the level of the manifest image: we want to deepen our romantic attachment to our partners or to reinvigorate a fading love. In order to do that when all traditional means have failed, we conceive of ourselves in a way that is suited only to the scientific image – as a collection of manipulable neurochemicals and malleable brain processes that we can tinker with in order to produce the results we want. But once we have started to conceive of ourselves in that way, it may be hard to regain the manifest-image conception of ourselves as a more or less fixed (within certain boundaries) particular person, which is something that we are required to be if we are to engage in loving relationships with other people. In aiming to gain control of our biology in the way that our authors think desirable, we see our everyday, empirical selves – the ones that we can manipulate – as nothing but a collection of sub-personal biological processes, and at the same time conceive of the self that can manipulate that collection as something featureless, indefinite, and resolutely non-particular.

Even if they do not want to deny (which, as we shall see shortly, they may well do) that possibility (2) actually obtains, our authors might object to what I have just had to say about the choosing self. They might want to claim that that self is far from featureless. Instead, they may argue, it embodies something both very definite and very personal, in the shape of our higher-order desires or, better still, our values. In making the sort of choice that Jamal makes with regard to his relationship with Joanna, we bring what is romantically salient to us into line with what we value in relationships. This sort of enterprise is at the heart of our authors' recommendation of love drugs. In using such drugs, we would not be harmonizing our recalcitrant biology with arbitrary choice, but with deeply held values that might be said to define us as the people we are. And if they do this, there can be no damaging loss of particularity in their use and so no violation of the dual-particularity requirement's second clause.

The trouble with this picture is that those deeply held values are portrayed as floating free of the romantically involved selves that we wish to manipulate in accordance with them, as if we could formulate such values independently of the factors that, in our actual relationships, we regard as reasons for love. Michael Hauskeller has a subtle argument that seems to address this very point:

> Couples, [our authors] argue should be allowed to pursue their 'highest values,' whatever they may be. We should be able to choose how much we want to love or not love, whom we love, and when we love, depending on what we think is important to our (own) lives. At the core of the whole proposal is ultimately a particular, liberal moral outlook that values individual autonomy over everything else. I sympathize with that. Like Earp and colleagues, I am very much in favor of upholding and promoting 'a person's ability to live her life "authentically" and in accordance with her goals and values' . . .. However, I am not convinced that we can identify those goals and values without taking into account how and what and whom we love.[101]

If I understand Hauskeller aright here, he is accusing the authors of putting the cart before the horse, in assuming that our highest values could be logically prior to, and in a fitting position to oversee and control, *ab initio*, what and whom our messy 'lower' selves love. But in fact, those higher values are merely an abstraction from what those messy selves love; and if they are not, then they have no definite content, and the choosing self is once again the featureless, non-particular self.

A distinct line of attack against our authors' position here might be adapted from C. S. Lewis's intriguing and prescient 1943 work, *The Abolition of Man*.[102] Note that if possibility (2) is actual, the use of love drugs manipulates, and thus alters, some of our reasons and values. It strong-arms us into valuing certain features of our partners that we had, perhaps, ceased to value, in the process changing our identity as agents in certain respects. Our authors, we are assuming, will tell us that we need not be concerned about this, as the alteration will be guided by higher-order reasons: what we value in a partner, in so to speak a first-order manner, will simply be brought into line with our second-order, more considered values. As a result, though we will alter ourselves in certain respects, that alteration will only make us more authentic, more ourselves.

A risk mentioned in Section 5 looms at this point – that the more considered values mentioned here may amount to no more than our valuing being in a relationship, with all the problems that we saw could accompany that. Even in the absence of that concern, however, Lewis warns us of a danger in the sort of thinking exemplified by our authors. That is, once we have started to see our reasons and values as essentially malleable – once, we might say, the scientific image of ourselves has been allowed to dominate – there is no reason to regard any of them as fixed or ultimate, even the 'higher-order' ones. They are all just things that can be mechanically manipulated. By coming to regard them in this way, we have in a sense come to stand outside them (again, perhaps as a featureless self). And, as Lewis tells us, 'those who stand outside all judgements of value cannot have any ground for preferring one of their own impulses to another except the emotional strength of that impulse'.[103] In other words, there is nothing left to guide the manipulation of reasons and values but mere desire, to which *all* reasons and values without exception thus end up becoming subordinate.

6.3 Assuming That Possibility (3) Obtains

We are still left, however, with possibility (3). This is the possibility that love drugs reveal to their takers reasons for attachment that they have had all along but have not appreciated as reasons. In other words, the idea is that the drugs work by producing, perhaps in tandem with conventional relationship therapy, insight into how things stand with regard to an agent's set of romantic reasons. It will be recalled that this was first considered as a possibility in Section 4.2, where we characterized it as a 'ground-clearing' interpretation of the action of love drugs. For the possibility to be actual, one or other version of the facilitative account would have to be true; as noted above, however, the truth of at least two versions of that account – the versions that see factor *F* as a pro-relationship mindset or as increased salience of certain stimuli – would not *entail* that the possibility obtains.

It seems to me that if possibility (3) were actual, *and we knew it to be actual*, there might be little to object to in the use of oxytocin to help strengthen attachment and save faltering relationships such as Jamal and Joanna's. Crucially, however, in order for the use of exogenous oxytocin for romantic purposes to be a desirable option, it would not be enough for possibility (3) to obtain. We would also need to *know* that it obtains.

To see why, let us suppose that possibility (3) as a matter of fact obtains: that Jamal takes oxytocin alongside relationship therapy; that he comes to regard considerations that authentically are reasons for him *as* reasons for him; and that his attachment to Joanna is put back on track. This would seem straightforwardly to be a good turn of events. However, unless Jamal and Joanna have strong reasons to suppose that possibility (3) is actual, rather than possibility (1) or possibility (2), they perhaps have not really benefited – or not benefited as fully as they might had their epistemic situation been different – from the way things have turned out. Joanna, for instance, will be in a comparable situation to Karen in Arrell's example concerning the use of Lupron alongside conventional relationship therapy. It will be recalled that Karen is in an unenviable epistemic state: she is inescapably uncertain whether Harry's new-found fidelity is a mechanical result of the Lupron he has taken – in which case he remains unchanged – or a result of a disposition-changing cognitive intervention. She is of course not delivered from that bind if the latter is in fact the case. Joanna will be mired in a similar uncertainty: she cannot be confident that she enjoys the intrinsic good of Jamal's love, because she does not know whether his reasons for being attached to her are his own (as will be the case if possibility (3) obtains) or not (as will be the case if possibility (2) obtains). Indeed, she cannot even be sure whether the considerations he cites for his attachment to her are any sort of reason at all, or simply *post hoc* rationalizations (as may be the case if possibility (1) obtains).

Jamal's epistemic status with regard to the reasons for his attachment – or lack thereof – will be similar to Joanna's. The considerations he cites may feel like reasons, and may feel as if they are genuinely *his* reasons, but it is hard to see how he can be sure that they are. He might be in a parallel position to Titania, encountered here addressing Bottom in a work by the British poet U. A. Fanthorpe:

> Privately, you should know my passion
> Wasn't the hallucination they imagined,
> Meddling king and sniggering fairy.
> You, Bottom, are what I love. That nose,
> Supple, aware; that muzzle, planted out
> With stiff, scratchable hairs; those ears,
> Lofty as bulrushes, smelling of hay harvest,
> Twitching to each subtle electric
> Flutter of the brain![104]

It seems to Titania, perhaps, that the potion has allowed her to understand for the first time that, for example, a creature's having ears that smell of hay harvest is a reason for her to be attached to him and has been such a reason all along. She may be convinced that the scales have fallen from her eyes. But should she be so sure? Could it not be that what she is now apprehending as a reason for attachment is in fact no such reason for her (though it may be for some creatures), but rather something she has been strong-armed into seeing as a reason by the action of the potion? Or could it be that, eloquent though her talk of a supple, aware nose, and so on is, it is really just a *post hoc* rationalization of something that she unaccountably, without any reason, feels? It would appear that she cannot know. Nor can Jamal know what is afoot in his own case. Not knowing, he should be, and probably naturally will be, circumspect about endorsing his attachment to Joanna, no matter how strong it seems to be.

In summary, then, whichever of possibilities (1)–(3) is actual, Jamal's use of exogenous oxytocin seems bound not to deliver a desirable state of affairs either for him or for Joanna. More precisely, though the obtaining of possibility (3) might be objectively desirable, any benefits it would have will be undermined by the fact that neither Jamal nor Joanna could ever be sure that it is actual.

Towards the end of Section 4, I said that we could afford to be agnostic about whether the accurate account of the action of endomimetic love drugs is the productive or the facilitative. Perhaps we can now see why: the news is not good whichever account we subscribe to. If the productive account is correct, then either possibility (1) obtains, and Jamal has attachment without reasons, or possibility (2) obtains and Jamal's reasons have somehow been mechanically produced along with his attachment. If on the other hand the facilitative account is correct, things are no better. Either possibility (2) or possibility (3) obtains, but Jamal (and Joanna) are epistemically in the dark about which is actual.

In this Element, I hope I have gone some way towards showing that our authors, and those who agree with their core argument, are a little precipitate in holding that there would be good reason to use endomimetic love drugs. There is at the very least some cause to be sceptical of that claim, and some counter-arguments – those put forward in Sections 5 and 6 – to be carefully considered before we can cheerfully embrace the brave new world that Earp, Savulescu, Sandberg, Wudarczyck, and Guastella see on the horizon. For now, though, it might be wise for us to carry on loving in the good old-fashioned way, secure in the knowledge that there are reasons for our attachments and that those reasons are our own.

Notes

1. Fisher 2004, Chapter 4.
2. In her book, Fisher lists these stages as lust, romantic love (or simply 'romance'), and attachment. The authors on whom we chiefly concentrate in the current work prefer to label the second stage 'attraction', and I follow that practice, chiefly because, as Carrie Jenkins comments, we presumably want to count long-term attachment as a species of romantic love. See Jenkins 2017, 23. Jenkins is also sceptical of the claim that love always progresses through these three stages. The asexual person in a loving relationship presumably does not pass through the 'lust' stage, and some people report that they are still in the 'attraction' phase decades into a relationship. There also seems to be no reason why the steadiness of attachment should not be present in some relationships from the very beginning. What is more, we may be sceptical of the notion that lust is a part of love. Instead, we may want to characterize it as, at best, a precursor to love and a non-necessary one at that.
3. Savulescu & Sandberg 2008.
4. Earp & Savulescu 2020, 67.
5. Earp, Sandberg, & Savulescu 2012, 562.
6. Earp & Savulescu 2020, 58.
7. Earp & Savulescu 2020.
8. Savulescu & Sandberg 2008, 36.
9. See for example Dos Santos, Bouso, Alcázar-Córcoles, & Hallak 2018.
10. Earp, Wudarczyk, Sandberg, & Savulescu 2013.
11. Earp & Savulescu 2020, 59–60; 66–7.
12. Jenkins 2017, 159.
13. McGee 2016, 81.
14. Arrell 2020.
15. Savulescu & Sandberg 2008, 37.
16. Earp, Sandberg, & Savulescu 2016, 766.
17. Earp, Sandberg, & Savulescu 2016, 766.
18. Hauskeller 2015, 363.
19. Earp, Savulescu, & Sandberg 2012.
20. Savulescu & Sandberg 2008, 33.
21. Earp, Sandberg, & Savulescu 2012, 583.
22. Earp, Sandberg, & Savulescu 2012, 571.
23. Savulescu & Sandberg 2008, 34–5.
24. Savulescu & Sandberg, 2008, 37.
25. Savulescu & Sandberg 2008, 37; Earp, Sandberg, & Savulescu 2012, 561–2.
26. Savulescu & Sandberg 2008, 37–8.
27. Earp, Sandberg, & Savulescu 2012.
28. Lopez-Cantero 2020, 157, n. 1.
29. Earp & Savulescu 2020, 79.
30. Earp & Savulescu 2020, 78.

31. Wudarczyk, Earp, Guastella, & Savulescu 2013, 476.
32. Savulescu & Earp 2014, 7.
33. Young 2009.
34. Savulescu & Earp 2014.
35. Earp, Wudarczyk, Sandberg, & Savulescu 2013, 4.
36. Earp, Wudarczyk, Sandberg, & Savulescu 2013, 4.
37. Though that is perhaps not *necessarily* the case: we might reasonably talk of the world described in the scientific image as *underlying* the world described in the manifest image, even though there are not two worlds here.
38. McGee 2016, 80.
39. Earp & Savulescu 2016, 94.
40. Strawson 2018, 130.
41. Strawson 2018, 142–3.
42. Strawson 2018, 145.
43. Jenkins 2017, 34.
44. Jenkins 2017, 34–5.
45. Jenkins 2017, 171–3.
46. Fisher 2004, 27.
47. Savulescu & Sandberg 2008, 39–40.
48. Fisher 2004, 49.
49. Earp & Savulescu 2020, 54.
50. Dummett 1991, 254.
51. Young 2009.
52. Fisher 2008.
53. Sellars 1963, 1–40.
54. Chappell 2017.
55. Chappell 2017, 710.
56. Sellars 1963, 20.
57. Savulescu & Sandberg 2008, 33. All emphases in the quotations in this paragraph are mine.
58. Earp, Sandberg, & Savulescu 2015, 324.
59. Liu & Wang 2003.
60. Savulescu & Sandberg 2008, 35.
61. Savulescu & Sandberg 2008, 37.
62. Jenkins 2017, 28.
63. Wudarczyk, Earp, Guastella, & Savulescu 2013, 479.
64. For example, Kosaka *et al.* 2012.
65. Wudarczyk, Earp, Guastella, & Savulescu 2013, 478.
66. Wudarczyk, Earp, Guastella, & Savulescu 2013, 478.
67. Wudarczyk, Earp, Guastella, & Savulescu 2013, 478.
68. Striepens *et al.* 2011, 445.
69. Nyholm 2015a.
70. Niko Kolodny, in a much-cited and ingenious paper, has argued that romantic love *just is* the valuing of a relationship. While this is an interesting and striking view, it is one that has not often been found convincing. Kolodny 2003.

71. Ferraro 2015, 486.
72. Ferraro 2015, 486.
73. hooks 2001.
74. Hauskeller 2015, 365.
75. Hursthouse 2001, Chapter 8. For Hursthouse's denial that a virtuous agent will be motivated by the thought of her own flourishing, see 180.
76. For an intriguing and persuasive account of this point, see Phillips 1970, Chapter 2.
77. Wolf 2015, 191.
78. Earp & Savulescu 2020, 188.
79. Spreeuwenberg & Schaubroeck 2020, 75.
80. Spreeuwenberg & Schaubroeck 2020, 74.
81. Murdoch 1997, 215.
82. Murdoch 1970, 52.
83. Wolf 2003.
84. McGee 2016, 89.
85. Earp & Savulescu 2020, 57–8.
86. Nyholm 2015a, 193.
87. Savulescu & Sandberg 2008, 34.
88. Savulescu & Sandberg 2008, 40.
89. Earp, Savulescu, & Sandberg 2015, 331.
90. What I have to say here is partially influenced by arguments made by Julian Dodd in denying that there is such a thing as a norm of truth. Dodd 2008, 149–55.
91. This fact is missed by one of Nyholm's critics, who portrays him as concerned with the value that love has for the lover: see Naar 2016.
92. Nyholm 2015b.
93. This account is found in Pettit 2015, Chapter 1.
94. Nyholm 2015a, 194.
95. Nyholm 2015a, 195.
96. Wudarczyk, Earp, Guastella, & Savulescu 2013, 478.
97. Pettit 2015, 24.
98. Montaigne 2004, 10.
99. Arrell 2018.
100. Arrell 2018, 402.
101. Hauskeller 2015, 364.
102. Lewis 2001.
103. Lewis 2001, 65–6.
104. Fanthorpe 2013, 79.

References

Arrell, Robbie. Should we biochemically enhance sexual fidelity? *Royal Institute of Philosophy Supplement* 83 (2018): 389–414.

Arrell, Robbie. No love drugs today. *Philosophy and Public Issues* 10 (2020): 45–60.

Chappell, Sophie Grace. The objectivity of ordinary life. *Ethical Theory and Moral Practice* 20 (2017): 709–21.

Dodd, Julian. *An Identity Theory of Truth*. Basingstoke: Palgrave Macmillan 2008.

Dos Santos, Rafael G., Bouso, José Carlos, Alcázar-Córcoles, Miguel Ángel, and Hallak, Jaime E. C. Efficacy, tolerability, and safety of serotonergic psychedelics for the management of mood, anxiety, and substance-use disorders: A systematic review of systematic reviews. *Expert Review of Clinical Pharmacology* 11 (2018): 889–902.

Dummett, Michael. Frege's myth of the third realm. In *Frege and Other Philosophers*. New York: Oxford University Press 1991: 249–62.

Earp, Brian D. and Savulescu, Julian. Is there such a thing as a love drug? Reply to McGee. *Philosophy, Psychiatry, and Psychology* 23 (2016): 93–6.

Earp, Brian D. and Savulescu, Julian. *Love Is the Drug: The Chemical Future of Our Relationships*. Manchester: Manchester University Press 2020.

Earp, Brian D., Sandberg, Anders, and Savulescu Julian. Natural selection, childrearing, and the ethics of marriage (and divorce): Building a case for the neuroenhancement of human relationships. *Philosophy and Technology* 25 (2012): 561–87.

Earp, Brian D., Sandberg, Anders, and Savulescu Julian. The medicalization of love. *Cambridge Quarterly of Healthcare Ethics* 24 (2015): 323–36.

Earp, Brian D., Sandberg, Anders, and Savulescu, Julian. The medicalization of love: Response to critics. *Cambridge Quarterly of Healthcare Ethics* 25 (2016): 759–71.

Earp, Brian D., Savulescu, Julian, and Sandberg, Anders. Love drugs and science reporting in the media: Setting the record straight. *Practical Ethics: Ethics in the News* 14 June 2012; http://blog.practicalethics.ox.ac.uk/2012/06/should-you-take-ecstasy-to-improve-your-marriage-not-so-fast/ (last accessed 15 November 2021).

Earp, Brian D., Wudarczyk, Olga A., Sandberg, Anders, and Savulescu, Julian. If I could just stop loving you: Anti-love biotechnology and the ethics of a chemical breakup. *American Journal of Bioethics* 13 (2013): 3–17.

Fanthorpe, U. A. Titania to Bottom. In *Selected Poems*. London: Enitharmon Press 2013.

Ferraro, David. On love, ethics, technology, and neuroenhancement. *Cambridge Quarterly of Healthcare Ethics* 24 (2015): 486–9.

Fisher, Helen. *Why We Love*. New York: Henry Holt and Company 2004.

Fisher, Helen. The brain in love. TED talk 2008; www.youtube.com/watch?v=OYfoGTIG7pY (last accessed 20 December 2021).

Hauskeller, Michael. Clipping the angel's wings: Why the medicalization of love may still be worrying. *Cambridge Quarterly of Healthcare Ethics* 24 (2015): 361–5.

hooks, bell. *All About Love: New Visions*. New York: Harper Collins 2001.

Hursthouse, Rosalind. *On Virtue Ethics*. New York: Oxford University Press 2001.

Jenkins, Carrie. *What Love Is*. New York: Basic Books 2017.

Kolodny, Niko. Love as valuing a relationship. *The Philosophical Review* 112 (2003): 135–89.

Kosaka, Hirotaka, Munesue, Toshio, Ishitobi, Makoto *et al.* Long-term oxytocin administration improves social behaviors in a girl with autistic disorder. *BMC Psychiatry* 12 (2012): 110.

Lewis, C. S. *The Abolition of Man*. New York: Harper Collins 2001.

Liu, Y., and Wang, Z. X. Nucleus accumbens oxytocin and dopamine interact to regulate pair bond formation in female prairie voles. *Neuroscience* 121 (2003): 537–44.

Lopez-Cantero, Pilar. Love by (someone else's) choice. *Philosophy and Public Issues* 10 (2020): 155–89.

McGee, Andrew. Is there such a thing as a love drug? *Philosophy, Psychiatry, and Psychology* 23 (2016): 79–92.

Montaigne, Michel de. *On Friendship*. London: Penguin 2004.

Murdoch, Iris. *The Sovereignty of Good*. London: Routledge & Kegan Paul 1970.

Murdoch, Iris. The sublime and the good. In *Existentialists and Mystics: Writings on Philosophy and Literature*. London: Penguin 1997: 205–20.

Naar, Hichem. Real-world love drugs: Reply to Nyholm. *Journal of Applied Philosophy* 33 (2016): 197–201.

Nyholm, Sven. Love troubles: Human attachment and biomedical enhancements. *Journal of Applied Philosophy* 32 (2015a): 190–202.

Nyholm, Sven. The medicalization of love and narrow and broad conceptions of human well-being. *Cambridge Quarterly of Healthcare Ethics* 24 (2015b): 337–46.

Pettit, Philip. *The Robust Demands of the Good: Ethics with Attachment, Virtue, and Respect*. Oxford: Oxford University Press 2015.

Phillips, D. Z. *Death and Immortality*. Basingstoke: Macmillan 1970.

Savulescu, Julian, and Earp, Brian D. Neuroreductionism about sex and love. *Think* 13 (2014): 7–12.

Savulescu, Julian, and Sandberg, Anders. Neuroenhancement of love and marriage: The chemicals between us. *Neuroethics* 1 (2008): 31–44.

Sellars. Wilfrid. Philosophy and the scientific image of man. In *Science, Perception and Reality*. London: Routledge & Kegan Paul 1963: 1–40.

Spreeuwenberg, Lotte and Schaubroeck, Katrien. The non-individualistic and social dimension of love drugs. *Philosophy and Public Issues* 10 (2020): 67–92.

Strawson, Galen. The silliest claim. In *Things that Bother Me: Death, Freedom, the Self, etc*. New York: New York Review Books 2018: 130–53.

Striepens, Nadine, Kendrick, Keith M., Maier, Wolfgang, and Hurlemann, René. Prosocial effects of oxytocin and clinical evidence for its therapeutic potential. *Frontiers in Neuroendocrinology* 32 (2011): 426–50.

Wolf, Susan. Sanity and the metaphysics of responsibility. In Watson, Gary (ed.), *Free Will*, 2nd ed. New York: Oxford University Press 2003: 372–87.

Wolf, Susan. The importance of love. In *The Variety of Values: Essays on Morality, Meaning, and Love*. New York: Oxford University Press 2015: 181–95.

Wudarczyk, Olga A., Earp, Brian D., Guastella, Adam, and Savulescu, Julian. Could intranasal oxytocin be used to enhance relationships? Research imperatives, clinical policy, and ethical considerations. *Current Opinion in Psychiatry* 26 (2013): 474–84.

Young, Larry J. Love: Neuroscience reveals all. *Nature* 457 (2009): 148.

Acknowledgements

My thanks are due to the Faculty of Culture and Creative Industries at the University of Central Lancashire for awarding me a sabbatical in the first semester of the 2021/22 academic year, which enabled me to carry out the bulk of work on this Element. I am also grateful to Alinda and Robert, whose wonderfully serene holiday accommodation in Powys provided the perfect distraction-free environment in which to kickstart the writing process. And thanks, as always, to the HKs for their support. The Element is dedicated, with love, to the memory of my brother Roy Kelly.

Cambridge Elements

Bioethics and Neuroethics

Thomasine Kushner

California Pacific Medical Center, San Francisco

Thomasine Kushner, PhD, is the founding Editor of the *Cambridge Quarterly of Healthcare Ethics* and coordinates the International Bioethics Retreat, where bioethicists share their current research projects, the Cambridge Consortium for Bioethics Education, a growing network of global bioethics educators, and the Cambridge-ICM Neuroethics Network, which provides a setting for leading brain scientists and ethicists to learn from each other.

About the Series

Bioethics and neuroethics play pivotal roles in today's debates in philosophy, science, law, and health policy. With the rapid growth of scientific and technological advances, their importance will only increase. This series provides focused and comprehensive coverage in both disciplines consisting of foundational topics, current subjects under discussion and views toward future developments.

Cambridge Elements ≡

Bioethics and Neuroethics

Elements in the series